A DISQUISITION ON GOVERNMENT

and Selections from the DISCOURSE

A reprint of the Liberal Arts Press edition of 1953,
with new Foreword and Bibliography by
Shannon C. Stimson

ISBN 0-87220-293-3 (paperback)
ISBN 0-87220-294-1 (hard cover)

Original ISBN 0-02-318280-6 (paperback)

John C. Calhoun

A DISQUISITION ON GOVERNMENT

and Selections from the DISCOURSE

Edited, with an introduction, by
C. GORDON POST
Frederick Ferris Thompson Professor
of Political Science
Emeritus, *Vassar College*

Foreword by
SHANNON C. STIMSON

Hackett Publishing Company, Inc.
Indianapolis/Cambridge

John C. Calhoun: 1782–1850

Copyright © 1953 by The Liberal Arts Press, Inc.
Reprinted 1995 by Hackett Publishing Company, Inc.

Foreword and New Selected Bibliography copyright © 1995
by Hackett Publishing Company, Inc.

07 06 05 04 03 02 01   2 3 4 5 6 7

For further information, please address
Hackett Publishing Company, Inc.
P.O. Box 44937
Indianapolis, Indiana 46244-0937

Cover design by Listenberger & Associates

ISBN 0-87220-293-3 paperback
ISBN 0-87220-294-1 hard cover

Library of Congress Catalog Card Number: 95-79153

The paper used in this publication meets the minimum requirements of
American National Standard for Information Sciences—Permanence of
Paper for Printed Library Materials, ANSI Z39.48-1984.

∞

CONTENTS

CALHOUN'S WRITINGS

FOREWORD
Changing Perspectives on John C. Calhoun

Just over forty years ago, C. Gordon Post contributed a succinct and important introduction to an edition comprising John C. Calhoun's *Disquisition on Government* and two excerpts from his voluminous *Discourse on the Constitution and Government of the United States.* Reading this introduction once again in the present edition, one is struck by the remarkable freshness of Professor Post's balanced exposition. Elements of Calhoun's early life, his vast and troubled experience at the highest levels of public office, and the exigencies of a Southern response to the Tariff Acts between 1828 and 1833 and to a growing Abolitionist movement in the North are presented as the essential context within which to comprehend Calhoun's controversial insights on the nature of man, the origins of government, and the doctrine of the concurrent majority.

Despite the fact that Calhoun's two major political treatises were published posthumously, his reputation and the character of his contribution as a theorist and practitioner of American politics were already contested in his lifetime, and the debate certainly did not end with his death in 1850. In this century, and notably since 1948, the year of Richard Hofstadter's famous characterization of Calhoun as the "Marx of the master class," the political and intellectual pendulum of Calhoun scholarship has continued to swing vigorously, encompassing a spectrum of interpretations of Calhoun ranging from reactionary conservative to pressure-group pluralist, from arch–political realist to hopeless political utopian, from committed unionist and ardent nationalist to states' rights advocate and divisive sectionalist, from spokesman for a variant of self-interested liberalism to that for a variant of the civic virtue tradition of classical republicanism.

The very fact that such a variety of interpretive schemata have been employed to characterize and interpret Calhoun's writings hints at something deeply problematic about the project of reevaluating his place in American political thought. Indeed, Calhoun's central premises seem to stand at odds with many of the fundamental principles of

America's constitutional tradition. His rejection of the primacy of the individual in politics in favor of the group, as well as his assertions that rights and duties were social in character and origin, that government was necessity based on fate rather than choice based on a trust, and that government's origins lay in war rather than contract, would seem to mark him as something of an outlier to the most basic premises of the American Revolution and the Constitution of the founding era. Yet Calhoun's empirical observation that the stability of American government did not rest at that time on the easily alternating, or fluidly shifting, majorities of Lockean individuals projected in *Federalist* 51 (and that it was never likely to do so) struck a resonant chord in the American experience. For Calhoun, as for Alexis de Tocqueville, this observation elicited a searing insight into the political potential of majoritarian democracies for creating permanent minorities over which a stable national legislative majority, irrespective of a bill of rights, might effectively exercise "absolute government" free of constitutional checks.

While Calhoun's own solutions to this problem—in the form of the doctrine of concurrent majority and the minority veto—drew superficial support from his historical excursus into the Roman Republic and Polish Diet, Professor Post recognizes that Calhoun argued with some success that these instruments already possessed legitimate, if informal, domestic roots in the very spirit of the American Constitution. Indeed, in interpreting the determination of the Constitutional Convention to keep slavery off the political agenda in Philadelphia and in viewing its patent refusal to interfere with existing slaveholding practices for fear of losing Southern ratification support as an informal exercise in concurrent majority decisionmaking, Calhoun was not wide of the mark. The subsequent arguments of Jefferson and Madison for state interposition, contained in the Kentucky and Virginia Resolutions of 1798, seemed to Calhoun only to reinforce his position on both the necessity for and the legitimacy of further formalizing the minority veto.

Ultimately, of course, Calhoun's strong theory of concurrent majority broke down over the issue of slavery in the immediate pre–Civil War context of the 1840s and 1850s.

America's earlier Constitutional "consensus" to ignore the institution of slavery had finally been extinguished. In its absence, there was little reason to believe in the power of a legal instrument such as Calhoun's minority veto to contribute to, much less to compel, compromise on a moral issue that now stood at the very heart of the sectional conflict. Since Calhoun's time, however, formal and informal variations of the doctrine of concurrent majority and the minority veto have been successfully employed both in a wide range of western European consociational democracies—such as Belgium, The Netherlands (1917–1967), Austria (1945–1966), and Switzerland—and in power-sharing experiments in Lebanon (1943–1975), in India, and in the constitution of post-apartheid South Africa.

The issue of the relative political power of minorities and majorities to pursue their interests in contemporary democracies, as well as the preservation and protection of the collective rights of linguistic, ethnic, cultural, and religious subpopulations within the modern state, remain of vital scholarly and practical significance to democratic thought. Indeed, it might even be argued that in many respects the practical playing out of disputes over these very issues has often shaped and directed the patterns of political development in democratic polities down to the present day. For this reason alone, the power and limitations of Calhoun's writings remain salient today.

SHANNON C. STIMSON

UNIVERSITY OF CALIFORNIA, BERKELEY
July, 1995

INTRODUCTION

John Caldwell Calhoun in April, 1845, informed a friend that he had commenced "an enquiry into the elements of political science, preliminary to a treatise on the Constitution of the U. States; but I know not whether I shall ever have time to finish it." Calhoun lived to complete the preliminary enquiry, *A Disquisition on Government*, and the treatise, *A Discourse on the Constitution and Government of the United States*, but he did not live to see either work in print.

The chief problem to which Calhoun gave his attention in both the *Disquisition* and the *Discourse* was how best to safeguard the interests and way of life of a minority against the will of democratic majorities.

The *Disquisition*, particularly, reveals Calhoun as a courageous and original thinker, as a keen observer and student of history, and possessed of insights beyond the ken of most of his contemporaries. Leaving aside the issue of slavery, Calhoun's thought displays a universality which will forever assure him a high position in the history of American political thought.

EDUCATION AND PUBLIC LIFE

Calhoun was born, March 18, 1782, in the Abbeville district in western South Carolina. He was the son of Scotch-Irish, Calvinist parents, Patrick and Martha Caldwell Calhoun. Patrick, tough, resourceful, and a man of strong convictions, was a leader in the community. He served as judge, surveyor, and member of the state legislature. He, like his son, was a strong individualist; he believed in a maximum of individual freedom consistent with social order. Patrick opposed the adoption of the Federal Constitution on the ground that the power with which the central government was to be endowed would prove destructive of liberty.

John Calhoun, in his early youth, had the benefit of little formal education. What education he had, however, was excellent. For a brief time he attended a log-cabin school, where he learned to read and to write and to do arithmetic. Later he attended the school of his brother-in-law, Moses Waddell, and here he received a strict classical education. Within two years he had prepared himself for Yale. He entered the college as a junior at the age of twenty and, again in two years, completed the requirements for the bachelor's degree. At Yale, Calhoun studied under the formidable Dr. Timothy Dwight, Yale's president, a Federalist, and at times a strong anti-unionist. Dr. Dwight was a bitter critic of Jefferson and his followers, and along with many other New Englanders in the early nineteenth century proposed secession as a solution for sectional conflict.

Following the two years in New Haven, Calhoun devoted more than a year to a study of law at the school in Litchfield, Connecticut. This institution, the first of its kind in America, was established in 1774 by Judge Tapping Reeve (Aaron Burr's brother-in-law), who was soon joined by Judge James Gould. Like Timothy Dwight, Reeve and Gould were ardent Federalists, disunionists even. Margaret Coit declares that

Not the South, not slavery, but Yale College and the Litchfield Law School made Calhoun a nullifier. In the little classroom, Reeve at white heat and Gould with cold logic argued the "right" of secession as the only refuge for minorities. Logically, their argument was unimpeachable. Messrs. Dwight, Reeve, and Gould could not convince the young patriot from South Carolina as to the desirability of secession, but they left no doubts in his mind as to its legality.[1]

Returning to South Carolina, Calhoun read more law and was admitted to the bar in 1807. Despite his success as a practising attorney, the law could not hold Calhoun; and during the years 1808 and 1809 he served his district in the state legislature. In 1810 he was elected representative to the Congress of the United States, and he continued a member of that

[1] Margaret L. Coit, *John C. Calhoun, American Portrait* (Boston, 1950), p. 42.

body until 1817. In Congress the Republican [2] Calhoun, manifesting considerable irritation over England's disregard of neutral rights, advocated war. He was at one with the War Hawks, Clay among them, who clamored for war and who succeeded in effecting a declaration of war, much to the chagrin and disappointment of commercial New England. In Congress, too, the Nationalist Calhoun supported the Tariff of 1816, declaring that the measure would form "a new and most powerful cement, far outweighing any political objections that might be urged against the system." [3]

Appointed Secretary of War by President Monroe, Calhoun from 1817 to 1825 did much to improve the military establishment of the United States. From 1825 to 1832, Calhoun was Vice-president, first under John Quincy Adams and then under Andrew Jackson. He resigned the Vice-presidency in order to represent South Carolina in the Senate. With the exception of a brief term as Secretary of State, Calhoun remained in the Senate until his death in 1850.

COTTON

In the meantime, there had been developments in the United States and elsewhere which turned Calhoun from a nationalist to a firm state rights advocate and finally a sectionalist.

First, cotton became an exceedingly profitable crop and,

[2] The term "Republican" as applied here must not be confused with the present-day Republican Party. In general, from 1789 to 1816, Federalists opposed state rights, localism, a strict interpretation of the Constitution, and the interests of agriculture. By 1816 the Federalists had all but disappeared as a party, and the Republicans alone controlled the destinies of the nation. In 1828, or thereabouts, two wings of the Republican Party emerged: the Democratic-Republican wing under the leadership of Andrew Jackson, the direct forerunner of the present-day Democratic Party, and the National-Republican wing under the leadership of Clay and Adams. From 1834 to 1854, the Whig Party, formed by a combination of National-Republicans and other groups, opposed the Democrats. Finally, in 1854, the present-day Republican Party was organized. Its first candidate for President was John C. Frémont (1856); its first successful candidate was Abraham Lincoln (1860).

[3] Gaillard Hunt, *John C. Calhoun* (Philadelphia, 1908), p. 29.

concurrently, slavery became a profitable institution. In the eighteenth century the extension of cotton cultivation was severely restricted by the lack of any rapid means of removing the cotton seed from the fiber. The seeds were removed either by hand or by means of rollers, but this was profitable only in connection with the long-fibered or sea-island variety which was cultivated along the seaboard. The short-fibered or inland variety of cotton yielded little profit, for the seeds were difficult to remove. Of course, the inland variety was grown, but in general only so much was raised as could be gathered and seeded by hand.[4] Eli Whitney, in 1793, invented the cotton gin, an absurdly simple device with which a slave could seed fifty pounds of cotton a day. This machine enabled planters to turn more and more land over to the cultivation of cotton.

Second, the new spinning and weaving machines of the eighteenth century—Kay's flying shuttle, Hargreaves' spinning jenny, Crompton's "mule," and the application of water and steam power to their operation—speeded the production of cotton cloth and made ever more urgent the demand for more and more raw cotton and cheap labor. The following figures [5] will indicate just what had taken place:

Years	Average Annual Production of Cotton in the U.S. in Pounds	Average Annual Exports of Cotton from the U.S. in Pounds	Percentage of Crops Exported
1791–95	5,200,000	1,738,700	33.43
1796–00	18,200,000	8,993,200	49.41
1801–05	59,600,000	33,603,800	56.38
1826–30	307,244,400	254,548,200	82.84
1831–35	398,521,600	329,077,600	82.57
1846–50	979,690,400	729,524,000	74.46
1856–60	1,749,496,500	1,383,711,200	79.51

[4] Ulrich Bonnell Phillips, *Life and Labor in the Old South* (Boston, 1929), Chs. VI, VII.

[5] Figures taken from *The South in the Building of the Nation* (Richmond, 1909), Vol. V, p. 211.

Third, westward expansion made slavery an overwhelming national issue. In 1789, a political equilibrium existed between the slave-holding and the free states; but the acquisition of Louisiana and Texas, the widespread use of the cotton gin and other textile machines, opened a large and fertile area to the "peculiar institution" and frequently jeopardized the equality of slave and free states in the Senate.

Fourth, the North developed industrially while in the South cotton culture expanded. Members of Congress from the North furthered protectionist policies, while Southern members, fearing retaliation from abroad, advocated lower duties on imports.

Thus an economic conflict was engendered between the North and the South, and it was over the Tariff Acts of 1828 and 1832 that South Carolina espoused the doctrine of nullification [6] and threatened secession.

State Rights and Nullification

Nullification was not born of this controversy. Nullification developed as a concomitant of the doctrine of state rights, which, in turn, had its genesis in the question of the nature of the union. Was the union intended to be a consolidated republic or a confederation of sovereign and independent states bound together by a formal compact, namely, the Constitution?

The state rights doctrine assumed several forms, depending upon circumstances. The most extreme statement of the doctrine, for example, held to the notion that the states did not relinquish their sovereignty when they agreed to enter the Union. When the people of each state, through especially elected conventions, chose to ratify the Constitution, they were accepting the limitations of that instrument as limitations upon their respective governments. This theory held that sovereignty did not reside in the state governments but

[6] The alleged right of a state of the Union to declare an Act of Congress inapplicable, null and void, and without force or effect, within its own borders.

in the people of the state, and that therefore what the people had given they may take away; that in no way was the sovereignty of the states diminished by the act of confederation. If the sovereign body elects to secede from the Union, there is nothing in the Constitution to prohibit it.

The state rights doctrine was also associated with the idea of a divided sovereignty. Hamilton, in the *Federalist*, asserted that "the plan of the convention aims only at a partial union or consolidation," the states clearly retaining "all the rights of sovereignty which they before had, and which were not, by that act, *exclusively* delegated to the United States." [7] And the United States Supreme Court, in *Chisholm* v. *Georgia*, decided in 1793, declared that the "United States are sovereign as to all the powers of government actually surrendered: each state in the Union is sovereign, as to all the powers reserved." [8] Who was to judge in case of conflict between the two sovereigns the Constitution did not specify; but many of the states, at one time or another, assumed that a decision in the matter rested with them.

Ten years after the adoption of the Constitution, Virginia and Kentucky adopted resolutions declaring the invalidity of the Alien and Sedition Acts.[9] The Virginia resolution,

[7] Modern Library ed., p. 194.

[8] 2 Dall. 419, 435.

[9] Determined to suppress the attacks upon them by the Republicans and to retain their hold on the powers of government, the Federalists unwisely enacted four measures known collectively as the Alien and Sedition Acts:

1. Extending from five to fourteen years the minimum period of residence in the United States before citizenship could be conferred upon an alien, and providing also for the registration of all white aliens arriving in the United States. (Act of June 18, 1798. 1 *Stat. L.* 566-569.)

2. Authorizing the President to deport all aliens whom he should judge to be dangerous to the peace and safety of the United States. (Act of June 25, 1798. 1 *Stat. L.* 570-572.)

3 Authorizing the President to order the arrest and deportation as alien enemies of all natives, citizens, and subjects of a foreign nation

fathered by James Madison, declared "explicitly and per-
emptorily" that the Assembly

... views the powers of the Federal Government as resulting
from the compact, to which the States are parties; as limited
by the plain sense and intention of the instrument constituting that compact; as no further valid than they are authorized
by the grants enumerated in that compact; and that in case of
a deliberate, palpable and dangerous exercise of other powers
not granted by the said compact, the States who are parties
thereto have the right, and are in duty bound, to interpose for
arresting the progress of the evil, and for maintaining within
their respective limits, the authorities, rights and liberties
appertaining to them.[10]

Jefferson urged an even stronger statement from the Kentucky legislature. That body resolved that the Federal Government was not "the exclusive or final *judge* of the extent of
the powers delegated to itself, since that would have made its
discretion, and not the Constitution, the measure of its
powers." [11] The resolution asserted that each party to the
compact had an equal right to determine for itself whether the
terms of the compact had been violated and the proper remedy
to be invoked. The Alien and Sedition Acts were declared to
be gross violations of the Constitution, and therefore void.

The state rights doctrine found expression not alone in the
South. For example, the Embargo of 1807 was adjudged by
the legislature of Massachusetts to be "unjust, oppressive and
unconstitutional, and not legally binding on the citizens of this

---

with whom the United States was at war. (Act of July 6, 1798.
1 *Stat. L.* 577-578.)

4. Providing severe penalties for anyone who, with intent to defame
or to bring into contempt or disrepute, should utter or write false,
scandalous, or malicious statements against the Government of the
United States or its officers; or who should combine or conspire with
others to oppose any duly constituted measures of the Government.
(Act of July 14, 1798. 1 *Stat. L.* 596-597.)

10 *The Writings of James Madison* (New York, 1906), Vol. VI, p. 326.

11 Ethelbert Dudley Warfield, *The Kentucky Resolutions of 1798*
(New York, 1887), p. 76.

state." [12] When the Federal Government called out the state
militia to serve under Federal officers, the Connecticut legislature passed a resolution announcing that "the state of Connecticut is a FREE SOVEREIGN and INDEPENDENT state; that the
United States are a *confederacy* of states; that we are a confederated and not a consolidated republic"; [13] and that the
demand of the Federal Government was violative of the
Constitution.

In protest against the Tariff Act of 1828, Calhoun prepared
for a special committee of the South Carolina legislature
what is called the South Carolina *Exposition and Protest*.
Adopted by the state legislature, this document explicitly
asserted the legal right of a state of the Union to refuse obedience to a national act when the state deemed the act to be
contrary to the Constitution. As stated in the *Exposition*:

> If it be conceded, as it must be by every one who is the least
> conversant with our institutions, that the sovereign powers
> delegated are divided between the General and State Govern-
> ments, and that the latter hold their portion by the same tenure
> as the former, it would seem impossible to deny to the States
> the right of deciding on the infractions of their powers, and the
> proper remedy to be applied for their correction. The right
> of judging, in such cases, is an essential attribute of sover-
> eignty—of which the States cannot be divested without losing
> their sovereignty itself—and being reduced to a subordinate
> corporate condition. [14]

But how is this remedy of nullification to be applied by the
states? In answer to this question, the *Exposition* rejects the
state legislature as the vehicle of nullification:

> It is sufficient that plausible reasons may be assigned against
> this mode of action, if there be one (and there is one) free
> from all objections. Whatever doubts may be raised as to the

---

[12] Quoted in Arthur Meier Schlesinger, *New Viewpoints in American
History* (New York, 1922), p. 224.

[13] *Ibid.*, p. 225.

[14] *Reports and Public Letters of John C. Calhoun*, edited by Richard
K. Crallé (New York, 1883), Vol. VI, p. 41.

question—whether the respective Legislatures fully represent the sovereignty of the States for this high purpose, there can be none as to the fact that a Convention fully represents them for all purposes whatever. Its authority, therefore, must remove every objection as to form, and leave the question on the single point of the right of the States to interpose at all. When convened, it will belong to the Convention itself to determine, authoritatively, whether the acts of which we complain be unconstitutional; and, if so, whether they constitute a violation so deliberate, palpable, and dangerous, as to justify the interposition of the State to protect its rights.[15]

The *Exposition* states clearly Calhoun's view of the effects of the Tariff Acts in the South; and it may be well, in order to comprehend better the *Disquisition*, to consider these effects as Calhoun understood them.

The Constitution gives to Congress the power to impose duties on imports for revenue; but this power is used by the majority, not only for revenue, but for the purpose "of rearing up the industry of one section of the country on the ruins of another"[16] and violating the Constitution in using a power for a legitimate object to accomplish another object, not legitimate. According to Calhoun:

So partial are the effects of the system, that its burdens are exclusively on one side and its benefits on the other. It imposes on the agricultural interest of the South, including the South-west, and that portion of the country particularly engaged in commerce and navigation, the burden not only of sustaining the system itself, but that also of the government.[17]

The South produced staples—cotton, rice, indigo—only one quarter of which were disposed of in the United States. The South was therefore an exporting section of the country, and her very life, her culture, her welfare, depended upon foreign markets. Producing staples primarily, the South was also a great importing section, and it was to her interest to buy abroad as cheaply as possible. The manufacturing North, on the other hand, fearing competition from abroad, pressed for

[15] *Ibid.*, pp. 44-45.   [16] *Ibid.*, p. 3.   [17] *Ibid.*, p. 5.

governmental protection. Thus the high duties specified in the Tariff Act of 1828 (and later in the Act of 1832) laid a heavy hand upon the South.

As the *Exposition* stated the matter, the South was required

... by the general competition of the world to sell *low*; and, on the other hand, by the Tariff to buy *high*. We cannot withstand this double action. Our ruin must follow. In fact, our only permanent and safe remedy is, not from the rise in the price of what we *sell*, in which we can receive but little aid from our Government, but a reduction in the price of what we *buy*; which is prevented by the interference of the Government.[18]

The *Exposition* also declared that, by means of the tariff, the South was contributing more than its fair share to the support of the general government and receiving an even more inadequate return in benefits. As Calhoun pointed out:

It has already been proved that our contribution, through the Custom-House, to the Treasury of the Union, amounts annually to $16,650,000, which leads to the inquiry—What becomes of so large an amount of the products of our labor, placed, by the operation of the system, at the disposal of Congress? One point is certain—a very small share returns to us, out of whose labor it is extracted . . . .[19]

The committee felt a thorough conviction, as a result of an examination of the annual appropriation acts,

... that a sum much less than two millions of dollars falls to our share of the disbursements; and that it would be a moderate estimate to place our contribution, above what we receive back, through all of the appropriations, at $15,000,000; constituting, to that great amount, an annual, continued, and uncompensated draft on the industry of the Southern States, through the Custom-House alone.[20]

Unsuccessful in effecting a reduction in the tariff rates in the Act of 1832, South Carolina, in convention, as proposed in the *Exposition*, adopted the Ordinance of Nullification.

[18] *Ibid.*, p. 21.   [19] *Ibid.*, p. 15.   [20] *Loc. cit.*

The Ordinance declared that "it shall not be lawful for any of the constituted authorities, whether of this State or of the United States, to enforce the payment of duties imposed by the said acts within the limits of this State"; [21] and concluded with a warning that any attempt on the part of the national government to enforce the tariff laws within the State of South Carolina would be

... inconsistent with the longer continuance of South Carolina in the Union; and that the people of this State will thenceforth hold themselves absolved from all further obligation to maintain or preserve their political connexion with the people of the other States, and will forthwith proceed to organize a separate government, and do all other acts and things which sovereign and independent States may of right do.[22]

State rights, nullification, and secession developed primarily from a profound conviction that an economic system and the way of life of a minority were endangered by a political majority. Madison had recognized the problem in the *Federalist*, Number 51: "If a majority be united by a common interest, the rights of the minority will be insecure." [23]

The Ordinance of Nullification met with little favorable response in the South, outside of South Carolina. President Jackson requested Congress to pass a "Force Bill" giving the Chief Executive the power to use the Army and Navy to enforce the collection of revenue in South Carolina. At the same time Jackson urged the Congress to reduce the tariff rates. The Tariff Act of 1833 brought lower duties, and South Carolina repealed the Ordinance of Nullification.

When Calhoun resigned the Vice-Presidency to take his seat in the Senate, he joined a group of men representative of a conscious and defensive minority. He sensed danger to the South in the constantly increasing population, the increasing financial, industrial, and political power, of the North. He saw the ties of finance binding North and West, and further

[21] *Niles' Register*, XLIII, p. 219.   [22] *Ibid.*, p. 220.
[23] Modern Library ed., p. 339.

isolating the South. He recognized the danger of William Lloyd Garrison [24] and his Abolitionists, and the attack upon slavery and the fugitive slave laws. He saw the Union that he loved departing more and more from the principles of federalism upon which it was originally based. He saw the ultimate impoverishment of the South and the destruction of its aristocracy and its slave system.[25] And for the rest of his life he fought, ever more bitterly in a losing battle, all measures designed to strengthen the nationalism of the period or to enhance the power of the central government or those measures which in any way threatened the interests of the minority of which he was so intimately and loyally a part.

He believed finally that the Union would survive only if a new political arrangement could be effected which would permit a balance of majority and minority interests.

And Calhoun, aware of the futility of the states' rights doctrine and nullification in the sense of the famous Ordinance, thought more in terms of sectional rights and interests and sectional nullification. It was in this connection that Calhoun set forth what he called the "doctrine of the concurrent majority." Thus we come to a consideration of *A Disquisition on Government*.

THE NATURE OF MAN

Recognizing the weakness of any system of government based upon unrealistic assumptions, Calhoun, in the *Disquisition*, almost immediately poses the question, "What is man?" From study and observation he assumed that man is a social being. Man's "inclinations and wants, physical and moral, irresistibly impel him to associate with his kind;

[24] William Lloyd Garrison (1805-1879) founder of the *Liberator* (1831) and the American Anti-Slavery Society (1833), was one of the most fearless and uncompromising leaders in the movement for the emancipation of the Negro population.

[25] See John Perry Pritchett, *Calhoun, His Defence of the South* (Poughkeepsie, 1937).

and he has, accordingly, never been found, in any age or country, in any state other than the social." [26]

Calhoun assumes, secondly, the inherent self-centeredness of man. Man is so constituted, says Calhoun, " that his direct or individual affections are stronger than his sympathetic or social feelings." He emphasizes that he purposely avoids use of the word "selfish," since this word "implies an unusual excess of the individual over the social feelings"—something "depraved and vicious"—and his intention is to "exclude such inference." This self-centeredness is a phenomenon of all "animated existence" and would seem to be connected "with the great law of self-preservation which pervades all that feels, from man down to the lowest and most insignificant reptile or insect." [27]

THE DENIAL OF SOCIAL CONTRACT

Calhoun assumes, thirdly, that while man is a social animal and incapable of the full development of his faculties outside of the social state, this state cannot exist without government. "In no age or country," Calhoun asserts, "has any society or community been found, whether enlightened or savage, without government of some description." [28] The reason for this is found in the second assumption, namely, the inherent self-centeredness of man. Man is the victim of man's suspicion, jealousy, anger, revenge; and this aspect of man must be controlled by government. But government cannot operate without men; government consists of men deciding and acting in the name of government; men who are subject to the same self-centeredness, the same passions, the same qualities, good and bad, as other men. Nonetheless, without government the existence of society would be jeopardized; without society, man's existence would be jeopardized. Thus, according to Calhoun, government has its origin in the fundamental nature of man, and not in some prehistoric contract.

[26] See page 3.   [27] See pages 4f.   [28] See pages 3f.

The idea of social contract as utilized by Hobbes, Locke, and Rousseau held that man lived originally in a state of nature. In general, man originally was a solitary, independent entity, free of rules and regulations except those imposed upon himself by himself. Each man in theory was his own lawmaker, his own judge, his own executive. Each man in theory possessed full, complete, and equal rights. Weary of his freedom or tired of the struggle of freeman against freeman, and in order to provide a greater freedom and security for all, men joined together by compact to form society. To do so, men agreed to divest themselves of certain of their natural rights—for example, the rights of individual lawmaking, individual judging, individual executing. These rights were given to society by means of the social contract; and society, by a second contract, entrusted these rights to those who would rule, the governors. But each man, having given up some of his natural rights, was still in possession of those not given, among them the inalienable rights of life, liberty, and the pursuit of happiness.

The contract theory, through Locke and Rousseau, exercised considerable influence on American political thought. The theory was invoked in the Declaration of Independence. It is accepted explicitly in the first article of the Constitution of New Hampshire (1784): "All men are born equally free and independent: therefore, all government, of right, originates from the people, is founded in consent, and instituted for the general good." The preamble of the Massachusetts' constitution (1790) declares that the purpose of government is to protect the body politic and

. . . to furnish the individuals who compose it with the power of enjoying in safety and tranquillity their natural rights, and the blessings of life; and whenever these great rights are not obtained, the people have a right to alter the government, and to take measures necessary for their safety, prosperity, and happiness.

Paine and Jefferson accepted the social contract theory; however, the former developed a corollary, namely, the doctrine of the periodic reaffirmation of natural rights. Jefferson said that "every constitution . . . and every law naturally expires at the end of thirty-four years" [29] (later he reduced the number to nineteen). Madison, also, assumed the contractual origins of political organization.

Calhoun denied the whole concept of social contract and natural rights, both of which had had long and respectable careers. Society, Calhoun argued, was not created by contract; society has always existed, and man has never existed outside of society. A state of nature, as described by the contract writers, never existed; nor were men ever endowed with natural rights. The only rights men have ever known were those granted by society. It was thus that Calhoun could repudiate equality and uphold slavery.

The Doctrine of the Concurrent Majority

"It is of great importance in a republic," declares James Madison in the *Federalist*, Number 51, "not only to guard the society against the oppression of its rulers, but to guard one part of society against the injustice of the other part." [30] Two methods are proposed to resolve the problem of minority insecurity. The first is "by creating a will in the community independent of the majority—that is, of the society itself." [31] This is rejected, however, since it would pertain only to governments possessing "an hereditary or self-appointed authority." The second method is not a method at all, but a hoped-for condition arising from the nature of a federal republic: "society itself will be broken into so many parts, interests and classes of citizens, that the rights of individuals, or of the minority, will be in little danger from interested combinations of the majority." [32] In little more than a quarter-century the South was to realize the futility of the second "method."

[29] Letter to James Madison, September 6, 1789, in *The Writings of Thomas Jefferson* (Washington, D. C., 1904), Vol. VII, p. 459.
[30] Modern Library ed., p. 339.   [31] *Loc. cit.*   [32] *Loc. cit.*

The means finally evolved by Calhoun by which majority and minority interests were to be more evenly balanced is called the "doctrine of the concurrent majority." The numerical majority consisting of men subject to the self-centeredness referred to above can be tyrannical and oppressive in the area of a self-centered minority's rights and interests. Calhoun proposed that each sectional majority or each major-interest majority should have the constitutional power to veto acts of the federal government, which represented the numerical majority, when those acts were deemed, by a majority of the people comprising the section or interest, to be adverse to the welfare of section or interest. It would be the will of a sectional majority acting concurrently with a numerical majority, the former endowed with the power to nullify the acts of the latter. Calhoun believed that this device would tend to unite

... the most opposite and conflicting interests and to blend the whole in one common attachment for the country. By giving to each interest, or portion, the power of self-protection, all strife and struggle between them for ascendancy is prevented; and thereby, not only every feeling calculated to weaken the attachment to the whole is suppressed, but the individual and social feelings are made to unite in one common devotion to country. Each sees and feels that it can best promote its own prosperity by conciliating the good will and promoting the prosperity of the others.[33]

The concurrent majority is designed "to enlarge and secure the bounds of liberty, because it is better suited to prevent government from passing beyond its proper limits, and to restrict it to its primary end—the protection of the community."[34]

To the argument that government could accomplish nothing under so pluralistic a system, and perhaps recalling the Ordinance of Nullification and the Tariff Act of 1833, Calhoun replied that in true constitutional government authority is upheld and preserved, not by force, but by compromise. The

[33] See pages 37-38.
[34] See pages 45-46.

different interests or sections would be compelled "to unite in such measures only as would promote the prosperity of all, as the only means to prevent the suspension of the action of the government; and, thereby, to avoid anarchy, the greatest of all evils." [35]

Though Calhoun was not specific as to the practical application of the doctrine of the concurrent majority, he believed it to be in no way impracticable. He believed that history afforded various examples of its concrete use: Rome, the Iroquois Confederacy, Poland, and Great Britain.

In Rome, during the later years of the Republic, the tribunes of the plebs could veto a proposal under discussion in the Senate when the proposal was deemed inimical to the interests of the plebs.[36]

The central government of the Iroquois Confederacy rested lightly upon the six nations. Each nation—Mohawks, Oneidas, Cayugas, Senecas, Onandagas, and Tuscororas—was sovereign and independent, and each worked with the others through the central government only when there was unanimity of opinion. When one of the nations opposed a step on the ground of threatened interests, nothing could be done. By persuasion and compromise agreement was reached which was considered to be advantageous to all.[37]

In Poland, during the seventeenth century, there developed a device designed to guarantee a most extreme liberty verging on anarchy. This was the *liberum veto*. Its basis appears to have been the notion of the absolute equality of each and every Polish gentleman, and this led directly to the conclusion that the unanimous vote of the Diet was required to approve proposed legislation. At first the veto was used moderately;

[35] See page 30.

[36] See Theodor Mommsen, *The History of Rome* (New York, 1887), Vol. I, pp. 345-371; also B. G. Niebuhr, *The History of Rome*, translated by Julius C. Hare and Connop Thirlwall (London, 1855).

[37] See Henry R. Schoolcraft, *Notes on the Iroquois* (New York, 1846); also Lewis H. Morgan, *League of the Ho-De-No-Sau-Nee or Iroquois* (New York, 1922).

but in time it came to be used more and more frequently, and with disastrous results. In 1652 an individual veto prevented a continuation of the Diet beyond the constitutional six weeks' period as requested by the king, in order that important matters of state might be considered. In 1681 the *liberum veto* handicapped the Polish king in his preparations for war against the Turks. The veto was abolished in 1791.[38]

Calhoun distinguished three estates in English government: King, Lords, and Commons. The King as a practical matter was subordinate to Parliament, but he nonetheless stood as a symbol of a tax-consuming and appointing interest—an executive interest, and as such an estate. Thus the Lords with their special interests, the Commons with their special interests, and finally the King with his special interests faced each other, each empowered to veto, each exercising a concurrent action, and all reaching agreement as a result of compromise.[39]

Calhoun found manifestations of the doctrine in the separation of powers, checks and balances, and in the process of amending the Constitution of the United States. To change the Constitution formally, it is necessary for at least three-fourths of the States to approve a proposed amendment, a majority large enough to allow a significant minority to forestall the will of the majority.

EVALUATION

Calhoun holds in the *Disquisition* that—

The necessary consequence of taking the sense of the community is . . . to give to each interest or portion of the community a negative on the others. It is this mutual negative among its various conflicting interests which invests each with

[38] *The Cambridge History of Poland,* edited by W. F. Reddaway (Cambridge, 1950), pp. 500, 514, 544-546.

[39] See in general George Burton Adams, *Constitutional History of England* (New York, 1921).

the power of protecting itself, and places the rights and safety of each where only they can be securely placed, under its own guardianship. Without this there can be no systematic, peaceful, or effective resistance to the natural tendency of each to come into conflict with the others: and without this there can be no constitution. It is this negative power, the power of preventing or arresting the action of the government, be it called by what term it may—veto, interposition, nullification, check, or balance of power—which, in fact, forms the constitution. They are all but different names for the negative power. In all its forms, and under all its names, it results from the concurrent majority. Without this there can be no negative, no constitution. . . . It is, indeed, the negative power which makes the constitution and the positive which makes the government. The one is the power of acting and the other the power of preventing or arresting action. The two, combined, make constitutional governments.[40]

Calhoun was aware of difficulty in arriving at the end set forth above. He was aware of difficulty in adapting formally the principle of the concurrent majority to the American constitutional system. He believed that in its operation it might be unwieldy. And he was none too clear as to the details of its practical application. To the South, comprising a closely knit group of states devoted almost exclusively to the production of cotton, the principle could have applied readily enough. But Calhoun, although concerned primarily with the South as a sectional interest, contemplated the device as a protection to other "major interests." Presumably other "major interests" would include finance and labor, manufacturing and cattle-raising, wheat-growing and shipping. How these interests would effectively exercise the principle of the concurrent majority, Calhoun does not make clear.

It is the conclusion of one writer, however, that the principle of the concurrent majority is "unwritten law" in the American political system; that it "is felt from the Presidency on down: in the nomination of candidates, the formation of cabinets, the operation of Congressional pressure groups, and

[40] See page 28.

so on; where 'availability' means the approval (and implied veto power) of every major group." [41]

"The concurrent veto in operation," says Charles M. Wiltse, "is a negative variation of the pressure group approach, which persists in one form or another in all diverse societies." [42] The American Federation of Labor, the National Association of Manufacturers, the American Bankers Association, the National Grange, the American Medical Association, the American Bar Association, and their respective state and local organizations, are examples of the organized special interests which serve to protect their members by persuasion or other pressure-group methods for or against legislative intervention, state and national. "Is it not in this fashion," says Wiltse, "that we have come in our time to the public purchase and destruction of foodstuffs in order to raise prices to fantastic levels in the interest of a special group? Is it not thus that we have come to pay wages for work unperformed, and rent for land unused?" [43]

Time Magazine, in its issue of May 19, 1952, detected in Georgia Senator Richard Russell's bid for the Democratic Presidential nomination an effort on the part of the South to maintain a solid front in order to veto some other unacceptable candidate and to force a compromise on FEPC.[44] The

[41] Margaret L. Coit, "Calhoun and the Downfall of States' Rights," in *The Virginia Quarterly Review* (Spring, 1952), Vol. XXVIII, No. 2, p. 199.

[42] Charles M. Wiltse, *John C. Calhoun, Sectionalist,* 1840-1850 (New York, 1951), p. 426.

[43] *Loc. cit.*

[44] Fair Employment Practice Commission. President Truman, in his Message to Congress on Civil Rights, February 2, 1948, recommended that legislation be adopted which would prohibit discrimination in employment based on race, color, religion, or national origin: "The legislation should create a Fair Employment Practice Commission with authority to prevent discrimination by employers and labor unions, trade and professional associations, and Government agencies and employment bureaus." (*Congressional Record,* Eightieth Congress, second session, p. 928.)

rule, revoked in 1936, that a Democratic Presidential candidate must be nominated by a two-thirds vote of the Convention gave the South an effective weapon to forestall "unacceptable" candidacies. The Democratic Party, substituting majority rule for the two-thirds rule, has led the South to try another protective device, namely, the revolt. Senator Russell and the South knew that his bid for the nomination was futile, but as *Time* has it, "He is working to build up the South's old veto power . . . ," [45] that is, to build up sufficient strength to demand and secure negotiation and compromise with the majority of the party, and thus to nominate a candidate acceptable to the South. As *Time* says:

Calhounism survives in a great and much maligned American institution, the smoke-filled room, where party leaders can do what the ballot box cannot do: measure the intensity with which various groups will react for or against (especially against) certain proposals. The majority may be mildly in favor of a policy, and a minority (sectional or otherwise) may be fanatically against it. Under those circumstances, the American politician will often withhold support until he can find a way of placating the minority.[46]

The dark prophecies of John C. Calhoun as to the fate of the South at the hands of Northern financiers, industrialists, and political majorities came to pass with a vengeance. The conditions to which the Southern people were reduced by war and reconstruction, politically, socially, and economically, are well known and need no recounting here, but despite improvement the struggle between the two regions, which began long before the Civil War, continued. With the close of the military phase of the struggle, "The tyranny of unrestrained majorities was left to work its will in triumph." [47]

Nevertheless, the conditions against which Calhoun strove are reflected in a statement of Ex-Governor Ellis Gibbs Arnall of Georgia, in 1946:

[45] Courtesy of *Time*; copyright of Time, Inc., May 19, 1952.
[46] *Loc. cit.*   [47] Pritchett, *op. cit.*, p 38.

The discriminations against the Southern and Western regions
of our country must be abated, both in the freight rate differ-
entials that prevent their normal industrial development and
in the distribution of Federal funds for highways, education,
and public health. If these injustices are not remedied, the
people of the South and of the West will become no more than
hewers of wood and drawers of water to imperial masters in
the East.[48]

And Hodding Carter, a well-known Mississippi editor, wrote
in the same year: "Historically speaking, the South has some
good reasons to cherish a grudge [against the North] even
now. The grudge is, basically, that which any colonial, ex-
ploited people hold for the financial and political heart of
the empire." [49] Mr. Carter asserts that "Before the South
can conquer its bigotry, its people must be better educated,
better clothed, better fed and better paid." But, he continues, "Before these things can come, the South must rid
itself of the economic despotism imposed by the North's financial hold upon capital, by patent monopolies, by tariff penalties
and the rest of the enchaining restrictions." [50]

The great significance of Calhoun's major works is that
they comprise a memorial and guide to the age-old problem
of minorities. This problem extends back to the darkness of
man's beginnings; it persists today. Our own generation has
witnessed the degradation of the individual and the suppression
of minorities by predatory collectivist systems. Employing
fear, violence, and death as instruments of repression, the
Soviet Union, Mussolini's Italy, and Hitler's Germany stand
out as ugly manifestations of man's inhumanity to man. The
framers of the Constitution of the United States were fully
aware that a government supported by democratic majorities
could be as tyrannous and as arbitrary as any absolute

[48] "The Southern Frontier," in *The Atlantic Monthly* (September,
1946), Vol. CLXXVIII, No. 3 (September, 1946), p. 35.
[49] "Chips on Our Shoulder Down South," in *The Saturday Evening
Post*, Vol. CCXIX, No. 118 (November 2, 1946), p. 145.
[50] *Loc. cit.*

monarch or dictator; and the awareness of this danger by the people of the United States is reflected in its insistence upon the addition of a Bill of Rights to the Constitution. As Madison declared in the *Federalist*, "In framing a government which is to be administered by men over men, the great difficulty lies in this: you must first enable the government to control the governed; and in the next place oblige it to control itself." [51] Calhoun voices much the same idea when he says,

The powers which it is necessary for government to possess, in order to repress violence and preserve order, cannot execute themselves. They must be administered by men in whom, like others, the individual are stronger than the social feelings. And hence, the powers vested in them to prevent injustice and oppression on the part of others will, if left unguarded, be by them converted into instruments to oppress the rest of the community.[52]

Human rights are not grounded in contract; nor are they founded, as Calhoun would have us believe, on the rights that a given society at a given time recognizes; the rights of man have their basis rather in the nature of man, in human need, in the hopes and dreams and capabilities of the individual. And as men differ from one another, so must conditions exist which allow for difference. The recognition of diversity among men is implicit in the Bill of Rights.

In our own day, when men are overwhelmed by a feeling of insignificance and by the complexity of "big" government, when values are distorted by materialism and man's sense of direction is vague and indistinct, when conformity plays so important a role in the lives of men, when "men of good will" persistently look to government as a cure-all for social ills, when more and more peoples have succumbed to totalitarian regimes, then it seems right and proper for us to study Calhoun. For Calhoun thought in terms of the individual, and not in

[51] No. 51, Modern Library ed., p. 337.
[52] See page 7.

terms of mass-man; he thought in terms of man as he is, not as he ought to be or as Calhoun would have liked him to be; he thought in terms of principle, and not in terms of expediency. Granted the unworthiness of the defense of slavery, he nonetheless thought in terms of diversity and not a deadly conformity, and he expressed his thoughts boldly in behalf of diversity without fear of consequence. He stood forth as a man, an individual, self-poised and free.

C. GORDON POST

VASSAR COLLEGE
June, 1953

GENERAL CHRONOLOGY OF THE CALHOUN PERIOD

1781 Lord Cornwallis surrenders at Yorktown, Virginia.

1782 *Calhoun born in South Carolina, March 18.* Daniel Webster born in New Hampshire, January 18.

1783 Treaty of peace between Great Britain and the United States, Paris.

1787 Northwest Ordinance. Constitutional Convention, Philadelphia.

1789 George Washington, President of the United States. First Congress meets in New York, March 4.

1792 Eli Whitney invents the cotton gin.

1794 Jay's Treaty.

1797 John Adams, President of the United States.

1798 Alien and Sedition Acts. The Virginia and Kentucky Resolutions.

1800 John Brown born in Connecticut.

1801 Thomas Jefferson, President of the United States.

1802 *Calhoun enters Yale College.*

1803 Louisiana Territory acquired by the United States.

1804 *Calhoun graduates from Yale.*

1805-6 *Calhoun attends the law school in Litchfield, Connecticut.*

1806-8 *Calhoun practices law.*

1807 Embargo Act. Robert Fulton develops the first successful steam vessel.

1808-9 *Calhoun a member of the Legislature of South Carolina.*

1809 James Madison, President of the United States. Abraham Lincoln born in Kentucky, February 12.

1811   *Calhoun marries his cousin, Floride Bonneau Colhoun.*

1811-17   *Calhoun a member of the United States House of Representatives. Chairman, Committee on Foreign Relations.*

1812-14   War with Great Britain.

1816   *Calhoun supports protective tariff.*

1817   James Monroe, President of the United States.

1817-25   *Calhoun, Secretary of War.*

1820   The Missouri Compromise.

1823   Announcement of the Monroe Doctrine.

1825   John Quincy Adams, President of the United States. Erie Canal completed.

1825-32   *Calhoun, Vice-President of the United States.*

1828   *Calhoun prepares the South Carolina "Exposition and Protest" in opposition to the Tariff Act of 1828.*

1829   Andrew Jackson, President of the United States. The Peggy Eaton affair.

1830   Webster's reply to Hayne on the question of states' rights.

1831   *Calhoun's "Address to the People of South Carolina" elaborating his views on the nature of the Union.*

1832   Tariff Act. South Carolina's Ordinance of Nullification. Andrew Jackson's Nullification Proclamation.

1833   Debate in Senate on the Force Bill. Compromise tariff act. Ordinance of Nullification repealed.

1832-44   *Calhoun a member of the United States Senate.*

1837   Martin Van Buren, President of the United States.

1841   William Henry Harrison, President of the United States, dies one month after inauguration; succeeded by John Tyler.

1844-45 *Calhoun, Secretary of State.*

1845-50 *Calhoun a member of the United States Senate. At work on* A Disquisition on Government *and* A Discourse on the Constitution and Government of the United States.

1845 James Knox Polk, President of the United States. Texas annexed.

1846 Wilmot Proviso. Dred Scott, a slave, sues for his freedom in a Missouri court.

1846-48 War with Mexico

1849 Zachary Taylor, President of the United States.

1850 *Calhoun dies in Washington, D. C., March 31. Buried in St. Philip's Churchyard, Charleston, South Carolina.* Compromises of 1850. Fugitive Slave Law.

1853 Franklin Pierce, President of the United States.

1854 Kansas-Nebraska Act.

1857 James Buchanan, President of the United States. The United States Supreme Court decides the Dred Scott case.

1859 John Brown and his followers seize Harper's Ferry.

1860 Abraham Lincoln elected President of the United States. South Carolina secedes from the Union, December 20.

1861 Alabama, Arkansas, Florida, Georgia, Louisiana, Mississippi, North Carolina, Tennessee, Texas, and Virginia, secede. Abraham Lincoln inaugurated March 4. The attack on Fort Sumter. The President calls for 75,000 volunteers.

1861-65 The War between the States.

SELECTED BIBLIOGRAPHY

The only complete edition of Calhoun's writings is that edited by Richard K. Crallé, *The Works of John C. Calhoun*, which was first published in 1853 by D. Appleton & Company, New York, and reprinted in 1883. Following is a list of supplementary texts on Calhoun and his contribution to American democracy:

Anderson, John M., ed., *Calhoun, Basic Documents*. State College, Pennsylvania, 1952.

Coit, Margaret L., *John C. Calhoun, American Portrait*. Boston, 1950.

————, "Calhoun and the Downfall of States' Rights," in *The Virginia Quarterly Review*, Vol. XXVIII, No. 2.

Gabriel, Ralph Henry, *The Course of American Democratic Thought*. New York, 1940. Ch. IX.

Heckscher, Gunnar, "Calhoun's Idea of 'Concurrent Majority' and the Constitutional Theory of Hegel," in *The American Political Science Review*, Vol. XXXIII, No. 4.

Hofstadter, Richard, *The American Political Tradition and the Men Who Made It*. New York, 1948. Ch. IV.

Hunt, Gaillard, *John C. Calhoun*. Philadelphia, 1908.

Meigs, William M., *The Life of John Caldwell Calhoun*, 2 vols. New York, 1917.

Parrington, Vernon Louis, *Main Currents in American Thought*, Vol. II, pp. 69-82. New York, 1927.

Pritchett, John Perry, *Calhoun, His Defence of the South*. Poughkeepsie, 1937.

Spain, August O., *The Political Theory of John C. Calhoun*. New York, 1951.

Styron, Arthur, *The Cast-Iron Man, John C. Calhoun and American Democracy*. New York, 1935.

Wiltse, Charles M., *John C. Calhoun, Nationalist, 1782-1828*. New York, 1944.

————, *John C. Calhoun, Nullifier, 1829-1839*. New York, 1949.

————, *John C. Calhoun, Sectionalist, 1840-1850*. New York, 1951.

Von Holst, H., *John C. Calhoun*. Boston, 1883.

NEW SELECTED BIBLIOGRAPHY

Beer, Samuel H., *To Make a Nation*. Cambridge, 1993.

Current, Richard, *John C. Calhoun*. New York, 1963.

Freehling, William W., "Spoilsmen and Interests in the Thought and Career of John C. Calhoun," in *The Journal of American History*, Vol. 52, No. 1, 1965.

Foner, Eric, *Free Soil, Free Labor, Free Men: The Ideology of the Republican Party Before the Civil War*. Oxford, 1970.

Hartz, Louis, "South Carolina vs. the United States," in Daniel Aaron, ed., *America in Crisis*. New York, 1952.

————, *The Liberal Tradition in America*. New York, 1955.

Harrison, J. William, "Last of the Classical Republicans: An Interpretation of John C. Calhoun," in *Civil War History*, Vol. 30, No. 3, 1984.

Herzberg, Roberta, "An Analytic Choice Approach to Concurrent Majorities: The Relevance of John C. Calhoun's Theory for Institutional Design," in *The Journal of Politics*, Vol. 54, No. 1, 1992.

Hurst, James Willard, *Law and the Conditions of Freedom in the Nineteenth-Century United States*. Madison, 1956.

Kateb, George, "The Majority Principle: Calhoun and His Antecedents," in *Political Science Quarterly*, Vol. 84, No. 4, 1969.

Lijphart, Arend, *Democracies: Patterns of Majoritarian and Consensus Government in Twenty-One Countries*. New Haven, 1984.

Maier, Pauline, "The Road Not Taken: Nullification, John C. Calhoun, and the Revolutionary Tradition in South Carolina," in *South Carolina Historical Magazine*, Vol. 82, No. 1, 1981.

Meriwether, Robert L.; Hemphill, Edwin W.; and Wilson, Clyde N., eds., *The Papers of John C. Calhoun*. Columbia, 1959- .

Niven, John, *John C. Calhoun and the Price of Union*. Baton Rouge, 1988.

Putterman, Theodore L., "Calhoun's Realism?" in *History of Political Thought*, Vol. XII, No. 1, 1991.

Rossiter, Clinton, *Conservatism in America*. New York, 1962.

NOTE ON THE TEXT

The present edition of *Calhoun's Disquisition on Government* and selections from *A Discourse on the Constitution and Government of the United States* is based on the earliest publication of these writings in *The Works of John C. Calhoun*, 1853, edited by Richard K. Crallé. The text follows the original except for minor editorial changes in spelling, capitalization, and punctuation. For the convenience of the reader, the editor has also supplied subheads, which are set in brackets.

O. P.

A DISQUISITION ON GOVERNMENT

A DISQUISITION ON GOVERNMENT

In order to have a clear and just conception of the nature and object of government, it is indispensable to understand correctly what that constitution or law of our nature is in which government originates, or to express it more fully and accurately—that law without which government would not and with which it must necessarily exist. Without this, it is as impossible to lay any solid foundation for the science of government as it would be to lay one for that of astronomy without a like understanding of that constitution or law of the material world according to which the several bodies composing the solar system mutually act on each other and by which they are kept in their respective spheres. The first question, accordingly, to be considered, What is that constitution or law of our nature without which government would not exist and with which its existence is necessary?

In considering this, I assume as an incontestable fact that man is so constituted as to be a social being. His inclinations and wants, physical and moral, irresistibly impel him to associate with his kind; and he has, accordingly, never been found, in any age or country, in any state other than the social. In no other, indeed, could he exist, and in no other— were it possible for him to exist—could he attain to a full development of his moral and intellectual faculties or raise himself, in the scale of being, much above the level of the brute creation.

I next assume also as a fact not less incontestable that, while man is so constituted as to make the social state necessary to his existence and the full development of his faculties, this state itself cannot exist without government. The assumption rests on universal experience. In no age or country has

3

any society or community ever been found, whether enlightened or savage, without government of some description.

Having assumed these as unquestionable phenomena of our nature, I shall, without further remark, proceed to the investigation of the primary and important question, What is that constitution of our nature which, while it impels man to associate with his kind, renders it impossible for society to exist without government?

The answer will be found in the fact (not less incontestable than either of the others) that, while man is created for the social state and is accordingly so formed as to feel what affects others as well as what affects himself, he is, at the same time, so constituted as to feel more intensely what affects him directly than what affects him indirectly through others, or, to express it differently, he is so constituted that his direct or individual affections are stronger than his sympathetic or social feelings. I intentionally avoid the expression *"selfish* feelings" as applicable to the former, because, as commonly used, it implies an unusual excess of the individual over the social feelings in the person to whom it is applied and, consequently, something depraved and vicious. My object is to exclude such inference and to restrict the inquiry exclusively to facts in their bearings on the subject under consideration, viewed as mere phenomena appertaining to our nature—constituted as it is; and which are as unquestionable as is that of gravitation or any other phenomenon of the material world.

In asserting that our individual are stronger than our social feelings, it is not intended to deny that there are instances, growing out of peculiar relations—as that of a mother and her infant—or resulting from the force of education and habit over peculiar constitutions, in which the latter have overpowered the former; but these instances are few and always regarded as something extraordinary. The deep impression they make, whenever they occur, is the strongest proof that they are regarded as exceptions to some general and well-understood law of our nature, just as some of the minor powers of the material world are apparently to gravitation.

I might go farther and assert this to be a phenomenon not of our nature only, but of all animated existence throughout its entire range, so far as our knowledge extends. It would, indeed, seem to be essentially connected with the great law of self-preservation which pervades all that feels, from man down to the lowest and most insignificant reptile or insect. In none is it stronger than in man. His social feelings may, indeed, in a state of safety and abundance, combined with high intellectual and moral culture, acquire great expansion and force, but not so great as to overpower this all-pervading and essential law of animated existence.

But that constitution of our nature which makes us feel more intensely what affects us directly than what affects us indirectly through others necessarily leads to conflict between individuals. Each, in consequence, has a greater regard for his own safety or happiness than for the safety or happiness of others, and, where these come in opposition, is ready to sacrifice the interests of others to his own. And hence the tendency to a universal state of conflict between individual and individual, accompanied by the connected passions of suspicion, jealousy, anger, and revenge—followed by insolence, fraud, and cruelty—and, if not prevented by some controlling power, ending in a state of universal discord and confusion destructive of the social state and the ends for which it is ordained. This controlling power, wherever vested or by whomsoever exercised, is *Government*.

It follows, then, that man is so constituted that government is necessary to the existence of society, and society to his existence and the perfection of his faculties. It follows also that government has its origin in this twofold constitution of his nature: the sympathetic or social feelings constituting the remote, and the individual or direct the proximate, cause.

If man had been differently constituted in either particular —if, instead of being social in his nature, he had been created without sympathy for his kind and independent of others for his safety and existence; or if, on the other hand, he had been so created as to feel more intensely what affected others than what affected himself (if that were possible) or even had this supposed interest been equal—it is manifest that in either case there would have been no necessity for government, and that none would ever have existed. But although society and government are thus intimately connected with and dependent on each other—of the two society is the greater. It is the first in the order of things and in the dignity of its object; that of society being primary—to preserve and perfect our race—and that of government secondary and subordinate —to preserve and perfect society. Both are, however, necessary to the existence and well-being of our race and equally of divine ordination.

I have said, if it were possible for man to be so constituted as to feel what affects others more strongly than what affects himself, or even as strongly—because it may be well doubted whether the stronger feeling or affection of individuals for themselves, combined with a feebler and subordinate feeling or affection for others, is not in beings of limited reason and faculties a constitution necessary to their preservation and existence. If reserved—if their feelings and affections were stronger for others than for themselves or even as strong, the necessary result would seem to be that all individuality would be lost and boundless, and remediless disorder and confusion would ensue. For each, at the same moment intensely participating in all the conflicting emotions of those around him, would, of course, forget himself and all that concerned him immediately, in his officious intermeddling with the affairs of all others, which, from his limited reason and faculties, he could neither properly understand nor manage. Such a state of things would, as far as we can see, lead to endless disorder and confusion not less destructive to our race than a state of anarchy. It would, besides, be remediless—for government would be impossible or, if it could by possibility exist, its object would be reversed. Selfishness would have to be encouraged, and benevolence discouraged. Individuals would have to be encouraged by rewards to become more selfish, and deterred by punishments from being too benevolent; and this, too, by a government administered by those who, on the supposition, would have the greatest aversion for selfishness and the highest admiration for benevolence.

To the Infinite Being, the Creator of all, belongs exclusively the care and superintendence of the whole. He, in his infinite wisdom and goodness, has allotted to every class of animated beings its condition and appropriate functions and has endowed each with feelings, instincts, capacities, and faculties best adapted to its allotted condition. To man, he has assigned the social and political state as best adapted to develop the great capacities and faculties, intellectual and moral, with which he has endowed him, and has, accordingly, constituted him so as not only to impel him into the social state, but to make government necessary for his preservation and well-being.

[PROTECTION AGAINST THE ABUSE OF POWER BY GOVERNMENT]

But government, although intended to protect and preserve society, has itself a strong tendency to disorder and abuse of its powers, as all experience and almost every page of history testify. The cause is to be found in the same constitution of our nature which makes government indispensable. The powers which it is necessary for government to possess in order to repress violence and preserve order cannot execute themselves. They must be administered by men in whom, like others, the individual are stronger than the social feelings. And hence the powers vested in them to prevent injustice and oppression on the part of others will, if left unguarded, be by them converted into instruments to oppress the rest of the community. That by which this is prevented, by whatever name called, is what is meant by *constitution*, in its most comprehensive sense, when applied to *government*.

Having its origin in the same principle of our nature, *constitution* stands to *government* as *government* stands to

society; and as the end for which society is ordained would
be defeated without government, so that for which government
is ordained would, in a great measure, be defeated without
constitution. But they differ in this striking particular. There
is no difficulty in forming government. It is not even a matter
of choice whether there shall be one or not. Like breathing,
it is not permitted to depend on our volition. Necessity will
force it on all communities in some one form or another. Very
different is the case as to constitution. Instead of a matter
of necessity, it is one of the most difficult tasks imposed on
man to form a constitution worthy of the name, while to form
a perfect one—one that would completely counteract the tendency of government to oppression and abuse and hold it
strictly to the great ends for which it is ordained—has thus
far exceeded human wisdom, and possibly ever will. From
this another striking difference results. Constitution is the
contrivance of man, while government is of divine ordination.
Man is left to perfect what the wisdom of the Infinite ordained
as necessary to preserve the race.

With these remarks I proceed to the consideration of the
important and difficult question, How is this tendency of
government to be counteracted? Or, to express it more fully,
How can those who are invested with the powers of government be prevented from employing them as the means of
aggrandizing themselves instead of using them to protect and
preserve society? It cannot be done by instituting a higher
power to control the government and those who administer it.
This would be but to change the seat of authority and to make
this higher power, in reality, the government, with the same
tendency on the part of those who might control its powers
to pervert them into instruments of aggrandizement. Nor
can it be done by limiting the powers of government so as to
make it too feeble to be made an instrument of abuse, for,
passing by the difficulty of so limiting its powers without
creating a power higher than the government itself to enforce
the observance of the limitations, it is a sufficient objection
that it would, if practicable, defeat the end for which govern-

ment is ordained, by making it too feeble to protect and preserve society. The powers necessary for this purpose will ever prove sufficient to aggrandize those who control it at the expense of the rest of the community.

In estimating what amount of power would be requisite to secure the objects of government, we must take into the reckoning what would be necessary to defend the community against external as well as internal dangers. Government must be able to repel assaults from abroad, as well as to repress violence and disorders within. It must not be overlooked that the human race is not comprehended in a single society or community. The limited reason and faculties of man, the great diversity of language, customs, pursuits, situation, and complexion, and the difficulty of intercourse, with various other causes, have, by their operation, formed a great many separate communities acting independently of each other. Between these there is the same tendency to conflict —and from the same constitution of our nature—as between men individually; and even stronger, because the sympathetic or social feelings are not so strong between different communities as between individuals of the same community. So powerful, indeed, is this tendency that it has led to almost incessant wars between contiguous communities for plunder and conquest or to avenge injuries, real or supposed.

So long as this state of things continues, exigencies will occur in which the entire powers and resources of the community will be needed to defend its existence. When this is at stake, every other consideration must yield to it. Self-preservation is the supreme law as well with communities as with individuals. And hence the danger of withholding from government the full command of the power and resources of the state and the great difficulty of limiting its powers consistently with the protection and preservation of the community. And hence the question recurs, By what means can government, without being divested of the full command of the resources of the community, be prevented from abusing its powers?

The question involves difficulties which, from the earliest ages, wise and good men have attempted to overcome—but hitherto with but partial success. For this purpose many devices have been resorted to, suited to the various stages of intelligence and civilization through which our race has passed, and to the different forms of government to which they have been applied. The aid of superstition, ceremonies, education, religion, organic arrangements, both of the government and the community, has been, from time to time, appealed to. Some of the most remarkable of these devices, whether regarded in reference to their wisdom and the skill displayed in their application or to the permanency of their effects, are to be found in the early dawn of civilization—in the institutions of the Egyptians, the Hindus, the Chinese, and the Jews. The only materials which that early age afforded for the construction of constitutions, when intelligence was so partially diffused, were applied with consummate wisdom and skill. To their successful application may be fairly traced the subsequent advance of our race in civilization and intelligence, of which we now enjoy the benefits. For without a constitution—something to counteract the strong tendency of government to disorder and abuse and to give stability to political institutions—there can be little progress or permanent improvement.

[CONSTITUTIONAL GOVERNMENT]

In answering the important question under consideration it is not necessary to enter into an examination of the various contrivances adopted by these celebrated governments to counteract this tendency to disorder and abuse, nor to undertake to treat of constitution in its most comprehensive sense. What I propose is far more limited: to explain on what principles government must be formed in order to resist by its own interior structure—or to use a single term, *organism*—the tendency to abuse of power. This structure, or organism, is what is meant by constitution, in its strict and more usual sense; and it is this which distinguishes what are called "constitutional" governments from "absolute." It is in this strict and more usual sense that I propose to use the term hereafter.

How government, then, must be constructed in order to counteract, through its organism, this tendency on the part of those who make and execute the laws to oppress those subject to their operation is the next question which claims attention.

There is but one way in which this can possibly be done, and that is by such an organism as will furnish the ruled with the means of resisting successfully this tendency on the part of the rulers to oppression and abuse. Power can only be resisted by power—and tendency by tendency. Those who exercise power and those subject to its exercise—the rulers and the ruled—stand in antagonistic relations to each other. The same constitution of our nature which leads rulers to oppress the ruled—regardless of the object for which government is ordained—will, with equal strength, lead the ruled to resist when possessed of the means of making peaceable and effective resistance. Such an organism, then, as will furnish the means by which resistance may be systematically and peaceably made on the part of the ruled to oppression and abuse of power on the part of the rulers is the first and indispensable step toward *forming* a constitutional government. And as this can only be effected by or through the right of suffrage—the right on the part of the ruled to choose their rulers at proper intervals and to hold them thereby responsible for their conduct—the responsibility of the rulers to the ruled, through the right of suffrage, is the indispensable and primary principle in the *foundation* of a constitutional government. When this right is properly guarded, and the people sufficiently enlightened to understand their own rights and the interests of the community and duly to appreciate the motives and conduct of those appointed to make and execute the laws, it is all-sufficient to give to those who elect effective control over those they have elected.

I call the right of suffrage the indispensable and primary

principle, for it would be a great and dangerous mistake to suppose, as many do, that it is, of itself, sufficient to form constitutional governments. To this erroneous opinion may be traced one of the causes why so few attempts to form constitutional governments have succeeded, and why of the few which have, so small a number have had durable existence. It has led not only to mistakes in the attempts to form such governments, but to their overthrow when they have, by some good fortune, been correctly formed. So far from being, of itself, sufficient—however well guarded it might be and however enlightened the people—it would, unaided by other provisions, leave the government as absolute as it would be in the hands of irresponsible rulers; and with a tendency, at least as strong, toward oppression and abuse of its power, as I shall next proceed to explain.

The right of suffrage, of itself, can do no more than give complete control to those who elect over the conduct of those they have elected. In doing this, it accomplishes all it possibly can accomplish. This is its aim—and when this is attained, its end is fulfilled. It can do no more, however enlightened the people or however extended or well guarded the right may be. The sum total, then, of its effects, when most successful, is to make those elected the true and faithful representatives of those who elected them—instead of irresponsible rulers, as they would be without it; and thus, by converting it into an agency, and the rulers into agents, to divest government of all claims to sovereignty and to retain it unimpaired to the community. But it is manifest that the right of suffrage in making these changes transfers, in reality, the actual control over the government from those who make and execute the laws to the body of the community and thereby places the powers of the government as fully in the mass of the community as they would be if they, in fact, had assembled, made, and executed the laws themselves without the intervention of representatives or agents. The more perfectly it does this, the more perfectly it accomplishes its ends; but in doing so, it only changes the seat of authority without counteracting, in the least, the tendency of the government to oppression and abuse of its powers.

If the whole community had the same interests so that the interests of each and every portion would be so affected by the action of the government that the laws which oppressed or impoverished one portion would necessarily oppress and impoverish all others—or the reverse—then the right of suffrage, of itself, would be all-sufficient to counteract the tendency of the government to oppression and abuse of its powers, and, of course, would form, of itself, a perfect constitutional government. The interest of all being the same, by supposition, as far as the action of the government was concerned, all would have like interests as to what laws should be made and how they should be executed. All strife and struggle would cease as to who should be elected to make and execute them. The only question would be, who was most fit, who the wisest and most capable of understanding the common interest of the whole. This decided, the election would pass off quietly and without party discord, as no one portion could advance its own peculiar interest without regard to the rest by electing a favorite candidate.

But such is not the case. On the contrary, nothing is more difficult than to equalize the action of the government in reference to the various and diversified interests of the community; and nothing more easy than to pervert its powers into instruments to aggrandize and enrich one or more interests by oppressing and impoverishing the others; and this, too, under the operation of laws couched in general terms and which, on their face, appear fair and equal. Nor is this the case in some particular communities only. It is so in all— the small and the great, the poor and the rich—irrespective of pursuits, productions, or degrees of civilization; with, however, this difference, that the more extensive and populous the country, the more diversified the condition and pursuits of its population; and the richer, more luxurious, and dissimilar the people, the more difficult is it to equalize the action of the government, and the more easy for one portion of the community to pervert its powers to oppress and plunder the other.

Such being the case, it necessarily results that the right of suffrage, by placing the control of the government in the community, must, from the same constitution of our nature which makes government necessary to preserve society, lead to conflict among its different interests—each striving to obtain possession of its powers as the means of protecting itself against the others or of advancing its respective interests regardless of the interests of others. For this purpose, a struggle will take place between the various interests to obtain a majority in order to control the government. If no one interest be strong enough, of itself, to obtain it, a combination will be formed between those whose interests are most alike —each conceding something to the others until a sufficient number is obtained to make a majority. The process may be slow and much time may be required before a compact, organized majority can be thus formed, but formed it will be in time, even without preconcert or design, by the sure workings of that principle or constitution of our nature in which government itself originates. When once formed, the community will be divided into two great parties—a major and minor—between which there will be incessant struggles on the one side to retain, and on the other to obtain the majority and, thereby, the control of the government and the advantages it confers.

[THE POWERS OF GOVERNMENT]

So deeply seated, indeed, is this tendency to conflict between the different interests or portions of the community that it would result from the action of the government itself, even though it were possible to find a community where the people were all of the same pursuits, placed in the same condition of life, and in every respect so situated as to be without inequality of condition or diversity of interests. The advantages of possessing the control of the powers of the government, and thereby of its honors and emoluments, are, of themselves, exclusive of all other considerations, ample to divide even such a community into two great hostile parties.

In order to form a just estimate of the full force of these advantages, without reference to any other consideration, it must be remembered that government—to fulfill the ends for which it is ordained, and more especially that of protection against external dangers—must in the present condition of the world be clothed with powers sufficient to call forth the resources of the community and be prepared at all times to command them promptly in every emergency which may possibly arise. For this purpose large establishments are necessary, both civil and military (including naval, where, from situation, that description of force may be required), with all the means necessary for prompt and effective action, such as fortifications, fleets, armories, arsenals, magazines, arms of all descriptions, with well-trained forces in sufficient numbers to wield them with skill and energy whenever the occasion requires it. The administration and management of a government with such vast establishments must necessarily require a host of employees, agents, and officers—of whom many must be vested with high and responsible trusts and occupy exalted stations accompanied with much influence and patronage. To meet the necessary expenses, large sums must be collected and disbursed, and for this purpose heavy taxes must be imposed, requiring a multitude of officers for their collection and disbursement. The whole united must necessarily place under the control of government an amount of honors and emoluments sufficient to excite profoundly the ambition of the aspiring and the cupidity of the avaricious, and to lead to the formation of hostile parties and violent party conflicts and struggles to obtain the control of the government. And what makes this evil remediless through the right of suffrage of itself, however modified or carefully guarded or however enlightened the people, is the fact that, as far as the honors and emoluments of the government and its fiscal action are concerned, it is impossible to equalize it. The reason is obvious. Its honors and emoluments, however great, can fall to the lot of but a few, compared to the entire number of the community and the multitude who will seek to participate in them. But without this there is a reason which renders it impossible to equalize the action of the government so far as its fiscal operation extends—which I shall next explain.

[THE EFFECTS OF UNEQUAL TAXATION AND DISBURSEMENT]

Few, comparatively, as they are, the agents and employees of the government constitute that portion of the community who are the exclusive recipients of the proceeds of the taxes. Whatever amount is taken from the community in the form of taxes, if not lost, goes to them in the shape of expenditures or disbursements. The two—disbursement and taxation—constitute the fiscal action of the government. They are correlatives. What the one takes from the community under the name of taxes is transferred to the portion of the community who are the recipients under that of disbursements. But as the recipients constitute only a portion of the community, it follows, taking the two parts of the fiscal process together, that its action must be unequal between the payers of the taxes and the recipients of their proceeds. Nor can it be otherwise; unless what is collected from each individual in the shape of taxes shall be returned to him in that of disbursements, which would make the process nugatory and absurd. Taxation may, indeed, be made equal, regarded separately from disbursement. Even this is no easy task; but the two united cannot possibly be made equal.

Such being the case, it must necessarily follow that some one portion of the community must pay in taxes more than it receives back in disbursements, while another receives in disbursements more than it pays in taxes. It is, then, manifest, taking the whole process together, that taxes must be, in effect, bounties to that portion of the community which receives more in disbursements than it pays in taxes, while to the other which pays in taxes more than it receives in disbursements they are taxes in reality—burthens instead of bounties. This consequence is unavoidable. It results from the nature of the process, be the taxes ever so equally laid and the disbursements ever so fairly made in reference to the public service.

It is assumed, in coming to this conclusion, that the disbursements are made within the community. The reasons assigned would not be applicable if the proceeds of the taxes were paid in tribute or expended in foreign countries. In either of these cases the burthen would fall on all in proportion to the amount of taxes they respectively paid.

Nor would it be less a bounty to the portion of the community which received back in disbursements more than it paid in taxes because received as salaries for official services, or payments to persons employed in executing the works required by the government, or furnishing it with its various supplies, or any other description of public employment—instead of being bestowed gratuitously. It is the disbursements which give additional and, usually, very profitable and honorable employments to the portion of the community where they are made. But to create such employments by disbursements is to bestow on the portion of the community to whose lot the disbursements may fall a far more durable and lasting benefit —one that would add much more to its wealth and population —than would the bestowal of an equal sum gratuitously; and hence, to the extent that the disbursements exceed the taxes, it may be fairly regarded as a bounty. The very reverse is the case in reference to the portion which pays in taxes more than it receives in disbursements. With them profitable employments are diminished to the same extent, and population and wealth correspondingly decreased.

The necessary result, then, of the unequal fiscal action of the government is to divide the community into two great classes: one consisting of those who, in reality, pay the taxes and, of course, bear exclusively the burthen of supporting the government; and the other, of those who are the recipients of their proceeds through disbursements, and who are, in fact, supported by the government; or, in fewer words, to divide it into tax-payers and tax-consumers.

But the effect of this is to place them in antagonistic relations in reference to the fiscal action of the government and the entire course of policy therewith connected. For the greater the taxes and disbursements, the greater the gain of the one and the loss of the other, and vice versa; and consequently, the more the policy of the government is calculated to increase taxes and disbursements, the more it will be favored by the one and opposed by the other.

The effect, then, of every increase is to enrich and strengthen the one, and impoverish and weaken the other. This, indeed, may be carried to such an extent that one class or portion of the community may be elevated to wealth and power, and the other depressed to abject poverty and dependence, simply by the fiscal action of the government; and this too through disbursements only—even under a system of equal taxes imposed for revenue only. If such may be the effect of taxes and disbursements when confined to their legitimate objects— that of raising revenue for the public service—some conception may be formed how one portion of the community may be crushed, and another elevated on its ruins, by systematically perverting the power of taxation and disbursement for the purpose of aggrandizing and building up one portion of the community at the expense of the other. That it *will* be so used, unless prevented, is, from the constitution of man, just as certain as that it *can* be so used; and that, if not prevented, it must give rise to two parties and to violent conflicts and struggles between them to obtain the control of the government is, for the same reason, not less certain.

Nor is it less certain, from the operation of all these causes, that the dominant majority, for the time, would have the same tendency to oppression and abuse of power which, without the right of suffrage, irresponsible rulers would have. No reason, indeed, can be assigned why the latter would abuse their power, which would not apply, with equal force, to the former. The dominant majority, for the time, would in reality, through the right of suffrage, be the rulers—the controlling, governing, and irresponsible power; and those who make and execute the laws would, for the time, be in reality but *their* representatives and agents.

Nor would the fact that the former would constitute a

majority of the community counteract a tendency originating in the constitution of man and which, as such, cannot depend on the number by whom the powers of the government may be wielded. Be it greater or smaller, a majority or minority, it must equally partake of an attribute inherent in each individual composing it; and, as in each the individual is stronger than the social feelings, the one would have the same tendency as the other to oppression and abuse of power. The reason applies to government in all its forms—whether it be that of the one, the few, or the many. In each there must, of necessity, be a governing and a governed—a ruling and a subject portion. The one implies the other; and in all, the two bear the same relation to each other—and have, on the part of the governing portion, the same tendency to oppression and abuse of power. Where the majority is that portion, it matters not how its powers may be exercised—whether directly by themselves or indirectly through representatives or agents. Be it which it may, the minority, for the time, will be as much the governed or subject portion as are the people in an aristocracy or the subjects in a monarchy. The only difference in this respect is that in the government of a majority the minority may become the majority, and the majority the minority, through the right of suffrage, and thereby change their relative positions without the intervention of force and revolution. But the duration or uncertainty of the tenure by which power is held cannot, of itself, counteract the tendency inherent in government to oppression and abuse of power. On the contrary, the very uncertainty of the tenure, combined with the violent party warfare which must ever precede a change of parties under such governments, would rather tend to increase than diminish the tendency to oppression.

[THE CONCURRENT MAJORITY]

As, then, the right of suffrage, without some other provision, cannot counteract this tendency of government, the next question for consideration is, What is that other provision? This demands the most serious consideration, for of all the questions embraced in the science of government it involves a principle, the most important and the least understood, and when understood, the most difficult of application in practice. It is, indeed, emphatically that principle which *makes* the constitution, in its strict and limited sense.

From what has been said, it is manifest that this provision must be of a character calculated to prevent any one interest or combination of interests from using the powers of government to aggrandize itself at the expense of the others. Here lies the evil: and just in proportion as it shall prevent, or fail to prevent it, in the same degree it will effect, or fail to effect, the end intended to be accomplished. There is but one certain mode in which this result can be secured, and that is by the adoption of some restriction or limitation which shall so effectually prevent any one interest or combination of interests from obtaining the exclusive control of the government as to render hopeless all attempts directed to that end. There is, again, but one mode in which this can be effected, and that is by taking the sense of each interest or portion of the community which may be unequally and injuriously affected by the action of the government separately, through its own majority or in some other way by which its voice may be fairly expressed, and to require the consent of each interest either to put or to keep the government in action. This, too, can be accomplished only in one way, and that is by such an organism of the government—and, if necessary for the purpose, of the community also—as will, by dividing and distributing the powers of government, give to each division or interest, through its appropriate organ, either a concurrent voice in making and executing the laws or a veto on their execution. It is only by such an organism that the assent of each can be made necessary to put the government in motion, or the power made effectual to arrest its action when put in motion; and it is only by the one or the other that the different interests, orders, classes, or portions into which the community may be divided can be protected, and all conflict and struggle between them prevented—by rendering it impossible to put or to keep it in action without the concurrent consent of all.

Such an organism as this, combined with the right of suffrage, constitutes, in fact, the elements of constitutional government. The one, by rendering those who make and execute the laws responsible to those on whom they operate, prevents the rulers from oppressing the ruled; and the other, by making it impossible for any one interest or combination of interests, or class, or order, or portion of the community to obtain exclusive control, prevents any one of them from oppressing the other. It is clear that oppression and abuse of power must come, if at all, from the one or the other quarter. From no other can they come. It follows that the two, suffrage and proper organism combined, are sufficient to counteract the tendency of government to oppression and abuse of power and to restrict it to the fulfillment of the great ends for which it is ordained.

In coming to this conclusion I have assumed the organism to be perfect and the different interests, portions, or classes of the community to be sufficiently enlightened to understand its character and object, and to exercise, with due intelligence, the right of suffrage. To the extent that either may be defective, to the same extent the government would fall short of fulfilling its end. But this does not impeach the truth of the principles on which it rests. In reducing them to proper form, in applying them to practical uses, all elementary principles are liable to difficulties, but they are not, on this account, the less true or valuable. Where the organism is perfect, every interest will be truly and fully represented, and of course the whole community must be so. It may be difficult, or even impossible, to make a perfect organism—but, although this be true, yet even when, instead of the sense of each and of all, it takes that of a few great and prominent interests only, it would still, in a great measure, if not altogether, fulfill the end intended by a constitution. For in such case it would require so large a portion of the community, compared with the whole, to concur or acquiesce in the action of the government that the number to be plundered would be too few and the number to be aggrandized too many to afford adequate motives to oppression and the abuse of its powers. Indeed, however imperfect the organism, it must have more or less effect in diminishing such tendency.

It may be readily inferred, from what has been stated, that the effect of organism is neither to supersede nor diminish the importance of the right of suffrage, but to aid and perfect it. The object of the latter is to collect the sense of the community. The more fully and perfectly it accomplishes this, the more fully and perfectly it fulfills its end. But the most it can do, of itself, is to collect the sense of the greater number; that is, of the stronger interests or combination of interests, and to assume this to be the sense of the community. It is only when aided by a proper organism that it can collect the sense of the entire community, of each and all its interests—of each, through its appropriate organ, and of the whole through all of them united. This would truly be the sense of the entire community, for whatever diversity each interest might have within itself—as all would have the same interest in reference to the action of the government—the individuals composing each would be fully and truly represented by its own majority or appropriate organ, regarded in reference to the other interests. In brief, every individual of every interest might trust, with confidence, its majority or appropriate organ against that of every other interest.

[The Numerical versus the Concurrent Majority]

It results, from what has been said, that there are two different modes in which the sense of the community may be taken: one, simply by the right of suffrage, unaided; the other, by the right through a proper organism. Each collects the sense of the majority. But one regards numbers only and considers the whole community as a unit having but one common interest throughout, and collects the sense of the greater number of the whole as that of the community. The other, on the contrary, regards interests as well as numbers—considering the community as made up of different and conflicting interests, as far as the action of the government is concerned —and takes the sense of each through its majority or appropriate organ, and the united sense of all as the sense of the entire community. The former of these I shall call the numerical or absolute majority, and the latter, the concurrent or constitutional majority. I call it the constitutional majority because it is an essential element in every constitutional government, be its form what it may. So great is the difference, politically speaking, between the two majorities that they cannot be confounded without leading to great and fatal errors; and yet the distinction between them has been so entirely overlooked that when the term "majority" is used in political discussions, it is applied exclusively to designate the numerical—as if there were no other. Until this distinction is recognized and better understood, there will continue to be great liability to error in properly constructing constitutional governments, especially of the popular form, and of preserving them when properly constructed. Until then, the latter will have a strong tendency to slide, first, into the government of the numerical majority, and, finally, into absolute government of some other form. To show that such must be the case, and at the same time to mark more strongly the difference between the two in order to guard against the danger of overlooking it, I propose to consider the subject more at length.

[THE NUMERICAL MAJORITY NOT THE PEOPLE]

The first and leading error which naturally arises from overlooking the distinction referred to is to confound the numerical majority with the people, and this so completely as to regard them as identical. This is a consequence that necessarily results from considering the numerical as the only majority. All admit that a popular government, or democracy, is the government of the people, for the terms imply this. A perfect government of the kind would be one which would embrace the consent of every citizen or member of the community; but as this is impracticable in the opinion of those who regard the numerical as the only majority and who can perceive no other way by which the sense of the people can be taken, they are compelled to adopt this as the only true basis of popular government, in contradistinction to governments of the aristocratical or monarchical form. Being thus constrained, they are, in the next place, forced to regard the numerical majority as in effect the entire people; that is, the greater part as the whole, and the government of the greater part as the government of the whole. It is thus the two come to be confounded and a part made identical with the whole. And it is thus also that all the rights, powers, and immunities of the whole people come to be attributed to the numerical majority—and, among others, the supreme, sovereign authority of establishing and abolishing governments at pleasure.

This radical error, the consequence of confounding the two and of regarding the numerical as the only majority, has contributed more than any other cause to prevent the formation of popular constitutional governments and to destroy them even when they have been formed. It leads to the conclusion that in their formation and establishment nothing more is necessary than the right of suffrage and the allotment to each division of the community a representation in the government in proportion to numbers. If the numerical majority were really the people, and if to take its sense truly were to take the sense of the people truly, a government so constituted would be a true and perfect model of a popular constitutional government; and every departure from it would detract from its excellence. But as such is not the case, as the numerical majority, instead of being the people, is only a portion of them, such a government, instead of being a true and perfect model of the people's government, that is, a people self-governed, is but the government of a part over a part—the major over the minor portion.

But this misconception of the true elements of constitutional government does not stop here. It leads to others equally false and fatal, in reference to the best means of preserving and perpetuating them, when, from some fortunate combination of circumstances, they are correctly formed. For they who fall into these errors regard the restrictions which organism imposes on the will of the numerical majority as restrictions on the will of the people and, therefore, as not only useless but wrongful and mischievous. And hence they endeavor to destroy organism under the delusive hope of making government more democratic.

Such are some of the consequences of confounding the two and of regarding the numerical as the only majority. And in this may be found the reason why so few popular governments have been properly constructed and why, of these few, so small a number have proved durable. Such must continue to be the result so long as these errors continue to be prevalent.

[CONSTITUTIONAL LIMITATIONS INSUFFICIENT TO CHECK THE NUMERICAL MAJORITY]

There is another error, of a kindred character, whose influence contributes much to the same results: I refer to the prevalent opinion that a written constitution containing suitable restrictions on the powers of government is sufficient, of itself, without the aid of any organism—except such as is necessary to separate its several departments and render them independent of each other—to counteract the tendency of the numerical majority to oppression and the abuse of power.

A written constitution certainly has many and considerable advantages, but it is a great mistake to suppose that the mere insertion of provisions to restrict and limit the powers of the government, without investing those for whose protection they are inserted with the means of enforcing their observance, will be sufficient to prevent the major and dominant party from abusing its powers. Being the party in possession of the government, they will, from the same constitution of man which makes government necessary to protect society, be in favor of the powers granted by the constitution and opposed to the restrictions intended to limit them. As the major and dominant parties, they will have no need of these restrictions for their protection. The ballot box, of itself, would be ample protection to them. Needing no other, they would come, in time, to regard these limitations as unnecessary and improper restraints and endeavor to elude them with the view of increasing their power and influence.

The minor or weaker party, on the contrary, would take the opposite direction and regard them as essential to their protection against the dominant party. And hence they would endeavor to defend and enlarge the restrictions and to limit and contract the powers. But where there are no means by which they could compel the major party to observe the restrictions, the only resort left them would be a strict construction of the constitution—that is, a constitution which would confine these powers to the narrowest limits which the meaning of the words used in the grant would admit.

To this the major party would oppose a liberal construction —one which would give to the words of the grant the broadest meaning of which they were susceptible. It would then be construction against construction—the one to contract and the other to enlarge the powers of the government to the utmost. But of what possible avail could the strict construction of the minor party be, against the liberal interpretation of the major, when the one would have all the powers of the government to carry its construction into effect and the other be deprived of all means of enforcing its construction? In a contest so unequal, the result would not be doubtful. The party in favor of the restrictions would be overpowered. At first, they might command some respect and do something to stay the march of encroachment, but they would, in the progress of the contest, be regarded as mere abstractionists, and, indeed, deservedly if they should indulge the folly of supposing that the party in possession of the ballot box and the physical force of the country could be successfully resisted by an appeal to reason, truth, justice, or the obligations imposed by the constitution. For when these, of themselves, shall exert sufficient influence to stay the hand of power, then government will be no longer necessary to protect society, nor constitutions needed to prevent government from abusing its powers. The end of the contest would be the subversion of the constitution, either by the undermining process of construction—where its meaning would admit of possible doubt —or by substituting in practice what is called party-usage in place of its provisions, or, finally, when no other contrivance would subserve the purpose, by openly and boldly setting them aside. By the one or the other, the restrictions would ultimately be annulled and the government be converted into one of unlimited powers.

Nor would the division of government into separate and, as it regards each other, independent departments prevent this result. Such a division may do much to facilitate its operations and to secure to its administration greater caution and deliberation; but as each and all the departments—and, of course, the entire government—would be under the control of the numerical majority, it is too clear to require explanation that a mere distribution of its powers among its agents or representatives could do little or nothing to counteract its tendency to oppression and abuse of power. To effect this, it would be necessary to go one step further and make the several departments the organs of the distinct interests or portions of the community and to clothe each with a negative on the others. But the effect of this would be to change the government from the numerical into the concurrent majority.

[CONCURRENT MAJORITY ESSENTIAL TO CONSTITUTIONAL GOVERNMENT]

Having now explained the reasons why it is so difficult to form and preserve popular constitutional government so long as the distinction between the two majorities is overlooked and the opinion prevails that a written constitution, with suitable restrictions and a proper division of its powers, is sufficient to counteract the tendency of the numerical majority to the abuse of its power—I shall next proceed to explain, more fully, why the concurrent majority is an indispensable element in forming constitutional governments and why the numerical majority, of itself, must, in all cases, make governments absolute.

The necessary consequence of taking the sense of the community by the concurrent majority is, as has been explained, to give to each interest or portion of the community a negative on the others. It is this mutual negative among its various conflicting interests which invests each with the power of protecting itself, and places the rights and safety of each where only they can be securely placed, under its own guardianship. Without this there can be no systematic, peaceful, or effective resistance to the natural tendency of each to come into conflict with the others; and without this there can be no constitution. It is this negative power—the power of preventing or arresting the action of the government, be it called by what term it may, veto, interposition, nullification, check, or balance of power—which in fact forms the constitution. They are all but different names for the negative power. In all its forms, and under all its names, it results from the concurrent majority. Without this there can be no negative, and without a negative, no constitution. The assertion is true in reference to all constitutional governments, be their forms what they may. It is, indeed, the *negative* power which makes the constitution, and the *positive* which makes the government. The one is the power of acting, and the other the power of preventing or arresting action. The two, combined, make constitutional governments.

But as there can be no constitution without the negative power, and no negative power without the concurrent majority, it follows necessarily that, where the numerical majority has the sole control of the government, there can be no constitution, as constitution implies limitation or restriction—and, of course, is inconsistent with the idea of sole or exclusive power. And hence the numerical, unmixed with the concurrent, majority necessarily forms, in all cases, absolute government.

It is, indeed, the single or *one power* which excludes the negative and constitutes absolute government, and not the *number* in whom the power is vested. The numerical majority is as truly a *single power*—and excludes the negative as completely as the absolute government of one or of the few. The former is as much the absolute government of the democratic or popular form as the latter of the monarchical or aristocratical. It has, accordingly, in common with them the same tendency to oppression and abuse of power.

Constitutional governments, of whatever form, are, indeed, much more similar to each other in their structure and character than they are, respectively, to the absolute governments, even of their own class. All constitutional governments, of whatever class they may be, take the sense of the community by its parts—each through its appropriate organ—and regard the sense of all its parts as the sense of the whole. They all rest on the right of suffrage and the responsibility of rulers, directly or indirectly. On the contrary, all absolute governments, of whatever form, concentrate power in one uncontrolled and irresponsible individual or body whose will is regarded as the sense of the community. And hence the great and broad distinction between governments is not that of the one, the few, or the many, but of the constitutional and the absolute.

From this there results another distinction which, although secondary in its character, very strongly marks the difference between these forms of government. I refer to their respective conservative principle—that is, the principle by which they are upheld and preserved. This principle in constitutional governments is *compromise*; and in absolute governments is *force*, as will be next explained.

It has been already shown that the same constitution of man which leads those who govern to oppress the governed, if not prevented, will, with equal force and certainty, lead the latter to resist oppression when possessed of the means of doing so peaceably and successfully. But absolute governments, of all forms, exclude all other means of resistance to their authority

than that of force, and, of course, leave no other alternative to
the governed but to acquiesce in oppression, however great it
may be, or to resort to force to put down the government. But
the dread of such a resort must necessarily lead the government to prepare to meet force in order to protect itself, and
hence, of necessity, force becomes the conservative principle
of all such governments.

On the contrary, the government of the concurrent majority,
where the organism is perfect, excludes the possibility of
oppression by giving to each interest, or portion, or order—
where there are established classes—the means of protecting
itself by its negative against all measures calculated to
advance the peculiar interests of others at its expense. Its
effect, then, is to cause the different interests, portions, or
orders, as the case may be, to desist from attempting to adopt
any measure calculated to promote the prosperity of one, or
more, by sacrificing that of others: and thus to force them
to unite in such measures only as would promote the prosperity
of all, as the only means to prevent the suspension of the
action of the government, and, thereby, to avoid anarchy, the
greatest of all evils. It is by means of such authorized and
effectual resistance that oppression is prevented and the necessity of resorting to force superseded in governments of the
concurrent majority; and hence compromise, instead of force,
becomes their conservative principle.

It would, perhaps, be more strictly correct to trace the conservative principle of constitutional governments to the necessity which compels the different interests, or portions, or orders
to compromise—as the only way to promote their respective
prosperity and to avoid anarchy—rather than to the compromise itself. No necessity can be more urgent and imperious
than that of avoiding anarchy. It is the same as that which
makes government indispensable to preserve society, and is
not less imperative than that which compels obedience to
superior force. Traced to this source, the voice of a people—
uttered under the necessity of avoiding the greatest of calamities through the organs of a government so constructed as to

suppress the expression of all partial and selfish interests, and to give a full and faithful utterance to the sense of the whole community, in reference to its common welfare—may, without impiety, be called *the voice of God*. To call any other so would be impious.

[TENDENCY TO ABSOLUTISM IN GOVERNMENT]

In stating that force is the conservative principle of absolute, and compromise of constitutional, governments, I have assumed both to be perfect in their kind, but not without bearing in mind that few or none, in fact, have ever been so absolute as not to be under some restraint, and none so perfectly organized as to represent fully and perfectly the voice of the whole community. Such being the case, all must, in practice, depart more or less from the principles by which they are respectively upheld and preserved, and depend more or less for support on force or compromise, as the absolute or the constitutional form predominates in their respective organizations.

Nor, in stating that absolute governments exclude all other means of resistance to its authority than that of force, have I overlooked the case of governments of the numerical majority which form, apparently, an exception. It is true that in such governments the minor and subject party, for the time, have the right to oppose and resist the major and dominant party, for the time, through the ballot box, and may turn them out and take their place if they can obtain a majority of votes. But it is no less true that this would be a mere change in the relations of the two parties. The minor and subject party would become the major and dominant party, with the same absolute authority and tendency to abuse power; and the major and dominant party would become the minor and subject party, with the same right to resist through the ballot box and, if successful, again to change relations, with like effect. But such a state of things must necessarily be temporary. The conflict between the two parties must be transferred, sooner or later, from an appeal to the ballot box to an appeal to force, as I shall next proceed to explain.

The conflict between the two parties, in the government of the numerical majority, tends necessarily to settle down into a struggle for the honors and emoluments of the government; and each, in order to obtain an object so ardently desired, will in the process of the struggle resort to whatever measure may seem best calculated to effect this purpose. The adoption by the one of any measure, however objectionable, which might give it an advantage, would compel the other to follow its example. In such case, it would be indispensable to success to avoid division and keep united; and hence, from a necessity inherent in the nature of such governments, each party must be alternately forced, in order to insure victory, to resort to measures to concentrate the control over its movements in fewer and fewer hands, as the struggle became more and more violent. This, in process of time, must lead to party organization and party caucuses and discipline, and these to the conversion of the honors and emoluments of the government into means of rewarding partisan services in order to secure the fidelity and increase the zeal of the members of the party. The effect of the whole combined, even in the earlier stages of the process, when they exert the least pernicious influence, would be to place the control of the two parties in the hands of their respective majorities, and the government itself virtually under the control of the majority of the dominant party, for the time, instead of the majority of the whole community —where the theory of this form of government vests it. Thus in the very first stage of the process the government becomes the government of a minority instead of a majority—a minority usually, and under the most favorable circumstances, of not much more than one-fourth of the whole community.

But the process as regards the concentration of power would not stop at this stage. The government would gradually pass from the hands of the majority of the party into those of its leaders, as the struggle became more intense and the honors and emoluments of the government the all-absorb-ing objects. At this stage principles and policy would lose all influence in the elections, and cunning, falsehood, deception, slander, fraud, and gross appeals to the appetites of the lowest and most worthless portions of the community would take the place of sound reason and wise debate. After these have thoroughly debased and corrupted the community, and all the arts and devices of party have been exhausted, the government would vibrate between the two factions (for such will parties have become) at each successive election. Neither would be able to retain power beyond some fixed term, for those seeking office and patronage would become too numerous to be rewarded by the offices and patronage at the disposal of the government; and these being the sole objects of pursuit, the disappointed would, at the next succeeding election, throw their weight into the opposite scale in the hope of better success at the next turn of the wheel. These vibrations would continue until confusion, corruption, disorder, and anarchy would lead to an appeal to force—to be followed by a revolution in the form of the government. Such must be the end of the government of the numerical majority, and such, in brief, the process through which it must pass, in the regular course of events, before it can reach it.

This transition would be more or less rapid, according to circumstances. The more numerous the population, the more extensive the country; the more diversified the climate, productions, pursuits, and character of the people, the more wealthy, refined, and artificial their condition; and the greater the amount of revenues and disbursements, the more unsuited would the community be to such a government, and the more rapid would be the passage. On the other hand, it might be slow in its progress amongst small communities during the early stages of their existence, with inconsiderable revenues and disbursements and a population of simple habits, provided the people are sufficiently intelligent to exercise properly the right of suffrage and sufficiently conversant with the rules necessary to govern the deliberations of legislative bodies. It is, perhaps, the only form of popular government suited to a people while they remain in such a condition. Any other would be not only too complex and cumbersome, but unnecessary to guard against oppression, where the motive to use power for that purpose would be so feeble. And hence colonies from countries having constitutional governments, if left to themselves, usually adopt governments based on the numerical majority. But as population increases, wealth accumulates, and, above all, the revenues and expenditures become large—governments of this form must become less and less suited to the condition of society until, if not in the meantime changed into governments of the concurrent majority, they must end in an appeal to force, to be followed by a radical change in its structure and character, and, most probably, into monarchy in its absolute form, as will be next explained.

Such, indeed, is the repugnance between popular governments and force—or, to be more specific, military power—that the almost necessary consequence of a resort to force by such governments, in order to maintain their authority, is not only a change of their form but a change into the most opposite—that of absolute monarchy. The two are the opposites of each other. From the nature of popular governments, the control of its powers is vested in the many, while military power, to be efficient, must be vested in a single individual. When, then, the two parties in governments of the numerical majority resort to force, in their struggle for supremacy, he who commands the successful party will have the control of the government itself. And hence, in such contests, the party which may prevail will usually find in the commander of its forces a master under whom the great body of the community will be glad to find protection against the incessant agitation and violent struggles of two corrupt factions—looking only to power as the means of securing to themselves the honors and emoluments of the government.

From the same cause, there is a like tendency in aristocratical to terminate in absolute governments of the monarchical form, but by no means as strong because there is less repugnance between military power and aristocratical than between it and democratical governments.

A broader position may, indeed, be taken; viz., that there is a tendency in constitutional governments of every form to degenerate into their respective absolute forms, and in all absolute governments into that of the monarchical form. But the tendency is much stronger in constitutional governments of the democratic form to degenerate into their respective absolute forms than in either of the others because, among other reasons, the distinction between the constitutional and absolute forms of aristocratical and monarchical governments is far more strongly marked than in democratic governments. The effect of this is to make the different orders or classes in an aristocracy or monarchy far more jealous and watchful of encroachment on their respective rights, and more resolute and persevering in resisting attempts to concentrate power in any one class or order. On the contrary, the line between the two forms, in popular governments, is so imperfectly understood that honest and sincere friends of the constitutional form not unfrequently, instead of jealously watching and arresting their tendency to degenerate into their absolute forms, not only regard it with approbation but employ all their powers to add to its strength and to increase its impetus, in the vain hope of making the government more perfect and popular. The numerical majority, perhaps, should usually be one of the elements of a constitutional democracy; but to make it the sole element, in order to perfect the constitution and make the government more popular, is one of the greatest and most fatal of political errors.

[The Concurrent Majority and Universal Suffrage]

Among the other advantages which governments of the concurrent have over those of the numerical majority—and which strongly illustrates their more popular character—is that they admit, with safety, a much greater extension of the right of suffrage. It may be safely extended in such governments to universal suffrage—that is, to every male citizen of mature age, with few ordinary exceptions; but it cannot be so far extended in those of the numerical majority without placing them ultimately under the control of the more ignorant and dependent portions of the community. For as the community becomes populous, wealthy, refined, and highly civilized, the difference between the rich and the poor will become more strongly marked, and the number of the ignorant and dependent greater in proportion to the rest of the community. With the increase of this difference, the tendency to conflict between them will become stronger; and as the poor and dependent become more numerous in proportion, there will be in governments of the numerical majority no want of leaders among the wealthy and ambitious to excite and direct them in their efforts to obtain the control.

The case is different in governments of the concurrent majority. There mere numbers have not the absolute control, and the wealthy and intelligent, being identified in interest with the poor and ignorant of their respective portions or interests of the community, become their leaders and protectors. And hence, as the latter would have neither hope nor inducement to rally the former in order to obtain the control, the right of suffrage, under such a government, may be safely enlarged to the extent stated without incurring the hazard to which such enlargement would expose governments of the numerical majority.

[CONCURRENT MAJORITY TENDS TO UNITE THE COMMUNITY]

In another particular, governments of the concurrent majority have greatly the advantage. I allude to the difference in their respective tendency in reference to dividing or uniting the community. That of the concurrent, as has been shown, is to unite the community, let its interests be ever so diversified or opposed, while that of the numerical is to divide it into two conflicting portions, let its interests be naturally ever so united and identified.

That the numerical majority will divide the community, let it be ever so homogeneous, into two great parties which will be engaged in perpetual struggles to obtain the control of the government has already been established. The great importance of the object at stake must necessarily form strong party attachments and party antipathies—attachments on the part of the members of each to their respective parties through whose efforts they hope to accomplish an object dear to all; and antipathies to the opposite party, as presenting the only obstacle to success.

In order to have a just conception of their force it must be taken into consideration that the object to be won or lost appeals to the strongest passions of the human heart—avarice, ambition, and rivalry. It is not then wonderful that a form of government which periodically stakes all its honors and emoluments as prizes to be contended for should divide the community into two great hostile parties; or that party attachments, in the progress of the strife, should become so strong among the members of each respectively as to absorb almost every feeling of our nature, both social and individual; or that their mutual antipathies should be carried to such an excess as to destroy, almost entirely, all sympathy between them and to substitute in its place the strongest aversion. Nor is it surprising that under their joint influence the community should cease to be the common center of attachment or that each party should find that center only in itself. It is thus that in such governments devotion to party becomes stronger than devotion to country—the promotion of the interests of party more important than the promotion of the common good of the whole, and its triumph and ascendency objects of far greater solicitude than the safety and prosperity of the community. It is thus also that the numerical majority, by regarding the community as a unit and having, as such, the same interests throughout all its parts, must, by its necessary operation, divide it into two hostile parts waging, under the forms of law, incessant hostilities against each other.

The concurrent majority, on the other hand, tends to unite the most opposite and conflicting interests and to blend the whole in one common attachment to the country. By giving to each interest, or portion, the power of self-protection, all strife and struggle between them for ascendency is prevented, and thereby not only every feeling calculated to weaken the attachment to the whole is suppressed, but the individual and the social feelings are made to unite in one common devotion to country. Each sees and feels that it can best promote its own prosperity by conciliating the good will and promoting the prosperity of the others. And hence there will be diffused throughout the whole community kind feelings between its different portions and, instead of antipathy, a rivalry amongst them to promote the interests of each other, as far as this can be done consistently with the interest of all. Under the combined influence of these causes, the interests of each would be merged in the common interests of the whole; and thus the community would become a unit by becoming the common center of attachment of all its parts. And hence, instead of faction, strife, and struggle for party ascendency, there would be patriotism, nationality, harmony, and a struggle only for supremacy in promoting the common good of the whole.

But the difference in their operation, in this respect, would not end here. Its effects would be as great in a moral as I have attempted to show they would be in a political point of view. Indeed, public and private morals are so nearly allied that it would be difficult for it to be otherwise. That which corrupts and debases the community politically must also corrupt and debase it morally. The same cause which in governments of the numerical majority gives to party attachments and antipathies such force as to place party triumph and ascendency above the safety and prosperity of the community will just as certainly give them sufficient force to overpower all regard for truth, justice, sincerity, and moral obligations of every description. It is, accordingly, found that in the violent strifes between parties for the high and glittering prize of governmental honors and emoluments— falsehood, injustice, fraud, artifice, slander, and breach of faith are freely resorted to as legitimate weapons, followed by all their corrupting and debasing influences.

In the government of the concurrent majority, on the

contrary, the same cause which prevents such strife as the means of obtaining power, and which makes it the interest of each portion to conciliate and promote the interests of the others, would exert a powerful influence toward purifying and elevating the character of the government and the people, morally as well as politically. The means of acquiring power —or, more correctly, influence—in such governments would be the reverse. Instead of the vices by which it is acquired in that of the numerical majority, the opposite virtues—truth, justice, integrity, fidelity, and all others by which respect and confidence are inspired—would be the most certain and effectual means of acquiring it.

Nor would the good effects resulting thence be confined to those who take an active part in political affairs. They would extend to the whole community. For of all the causes which contribute to form the character of a people, those by which power, influence, and standing in the government are more certainly and readily obtained are by far the most powerful. These are the objects most eagerly sought of all others by the talented and aspiring; and the possession of which commands the greatest respect and admiration. But just in proportion to this respect and admiration will be their appreciation by those whose energy, intellect, and position in society are calculated to exert the greatest influence in forming the character of a people. If knowledge, wisdom, patriotism, and virtue be the most certain means of acquiring them, they will be most highly appreciated and assiduously cultivated; and this would cause them to become prominent traits in the character of the people. But if, on the contrary, cunning, fraud, treachery, and party devotion be the most certain, they will be the most highly prized and become marked features in their character. So powerful, indeed, is the operation of the concurrent majority in this respect that, if it were possible for a corrupt and degenerate community to establish and maintain a well-organized government of the kind, it would of itself purify and regenerate them, while, on the other hand, a government based wholly on the numerical majority would just as certainly corrupt and debase the most patriotic and virtuous people. So great is their difference in this respect that just as the one or the other element predominates in the construction of any government, in the same proportion will the character of the government and the people rise or sink in the scale of patriotism and virtue. Neither religion nor education can counteract the strong tendency of the numerical majority to corrupt and debase the people.

[LIBERTY AND POWER THE OBJECTIVES OF GOOD GOVERNMENT]

If the two be compared in reference to the ends for which government is ordained, the superiority of the government of the concurrent majority will not be less striking. These, as has been stated, are twofold: to protect and to perfect society. But to preserve society, it is necessary to guard the community against injustice, violence, and anarchy within, and against attacks from without. If it fail in either, it would fail in the primary end of government and would not deserve the name.

To perfect society, it is necessary to develop the faculties, intellectual and moral, with which man is endowed. But the mainspring to their development and, through this, to progress, improvement, and civilization, with all their blessings, is the desire of individuals to better their condition. For this purpose liberty and security are indispensable. Liberty leaves each free to pursue the course he may deem best to promote his interest and happiness, as far as it may be compatible with the primary end for which government is ordained, while security gives assurance to each that he shall not be deprived of the fruits of his exertions to better his condition. These combined give to this desire the strongest impulse of which it is susceptible. For to extend liberty beyond the limits assigned would be to weaken the government and to render it incompetent to fulfill its primary end —the protection of society against dangers, internal and external. The effect of this would be insecurity; and of insecurity, to weaken the impulse of individuals to better their condition and thereby retard progress and improvement. On the other hand, to extend the powers of the government so as to contract the sphere assigned to liberty would have the same effect, by disabling individuals in their efforts to better their condition.

Herein is to be found the principle which assigns to power and liberty their proper spheres and reconciles each to the other under all circumstances. For if power be necessary to secure to liberty the fruits of its exertions, liberty, in turn, repays power with interest—by increased population, wealth, and other advantages which progress and improvement bestow on the community. By thus assigning to each its appropriate sphere, all conflicts between them cease, and each is made to cooperate with and assist the other in fulfilling the great ends for which government is ordained.

But the principle, applied to different communities, will assign to them different limits. It will assign a larger sphere to power and a more contracted one to liberty, or the reverse, according to circumstances. To the former, there must ever be allotted, under all circumstances, a sphere sufficiently large to protect the community against danger from without and violence and anarchy within. The residuum belongs to liberty. More cannot be safely or rightly allotted to it.

But some communities require a far greater amount of power than others to protect them against anarchy and external dangers; and, of course, the sphere of liberty in such must be proportionally contracted. The causes calculated to enlarge the one and contract the other are numerous and various. Some are physical—such as open and exposed frontiers surrounded by powerful and hostile neighbors. Others are moral—such as the different degrees of intelligence, patriotism, and virtue among the mass of the community, and their experience and proficiency in the art of self-government. Of these, the moral are by far the most influential. A community may possess all the necessary moral qualifications in so high a degree as to be capable of self-government under the most adverse circumstances, while, on the other hand, another may be so sunk in ignorance and vice as to be incapable of forming a conception of liberty or of living, even when most favored by circumstances, under any other than an absolute and despotic government.

The principle in all communities, according to these numerous and various causes, assigns to power and liberty their proper spheres. To allow to liberty, in any case, a sphere of action more extended than this assigns would lead to anarchy, and this, probably, in the end to a contraction instead of an enlargement of its sphere. Liberty, then, when forced on a people unfit for it, would, instead of a blessing, be a curse, as it would in its reaction lead directly to anarchy—the greatest of all curses. No people, indeed, can long enjoy more liberty than that to which their situation and advanced intelligence and morals fairly entitle them. If more than this be allowed, they must soon fall into confusion and disorder—to be followed, if not by anarchy and despotism, by a change to a form of government more simple and absolute, and therefore better suited to their condition. And hence, although it may be true that a people may not have as much liberty as they are fairly entitled to and are capable of enjoying, yet the reverse is unquestionably true—that no people can long possess more than they are fairly entitled to.

Liberty, indeed, though among the greatest of blessings, is not so great as that of protection, inasmuch as the end of the former is the progress and improvement of the race, while that of the latter is its preservation and perpetuation. And hence, when the two come into conflict, liberty must, and ever ought, to yield to protection, as the existence of the race is of greater moment than its improvement.

It follows, from what has been stated, that it is a great and dangerous error to suppose that all people are equally entitled to liberty. It is a reward to be earned, not a blessing to be gratuitously lavished on all alike—a reward reserved for the intelligent, the patriotic, the virtuous and deserving, and not a boon to be bestowed on a people too ignorant, degraded, and vicious to be capable either of appreciating or of enjoying it. Nor is it any disparagement to liberty that such is and ought to be the case. On the contrary, its greatest praise— its proudest distinction is that an all-wise Providence has reserved it as the noblest and highest reward for the development of our faculties, moral and intellectual. A reward more appropriate than liberty could not be conferred on the deserving, nor a punishment inflicted on the undeserving more just than to be subject to lawless and despotic rule. This dispensation seems to be the result of some fixed law; and every effort to disturb or defeat it, by attempting to elevate a people in the scale of liberty above the point to which they are entitled to rise, must ever prove abortive and end in disappointment. The progress of a people rising from a lower to a higher point in the scale of liberty is necessarily slow; and by attempting to precipitate, we either retard or permanently defeat it.

[Liberty and Equality]

There is another error, not less great and dangerous, usually associated with the one which has just been considered. I refer to the opinion that liberty and equality are so intimately united that liberty cannot be perfect without perfect equality.

That they are united to a certain extent, and that equality of citizens, in the eyes of the law, is essential to liberty in a popular government is conceded. But to go further and make equality of *condition* essential to liberty would be to destroy both liberty and progress. The reason is that inequality of condition, while it is a necessary consequence of liberty, is at the same time indispensable to progress. In order to understand why this is so, it is necessary to bear in mind that the mainspring to progress is the desire of individuals to better their condition, and that the strongest impulse which can be given to it is to leave individuals free to exert themselves in the manner they may deem best for that purpose, as far at least as it can be done consistently with the ends for which government is ordained, and to secure to all the fruits of their exertions. Now, as individuals differ greatly from each other in intelligence, sagacity, energy, perseverance, skill, habits of industry and economy, physical power, position and opportunity—the necessary effect of leaving all free to exert themselves to better their condition must be a corresponding inequality between those who may possess these qualities and advantages in a high degree and those who may be deficient in them. The only means by which this result can be prevented are either to impose such restrictions on the exertions of those who may possess them in a high degree as will place them on a level with those who do not, or to deprive them of the fruits of their exertions. But to impose such restrictions on them would be destructive of liberty, while to deprive them of the fruits of their exertions would be to destroy the desire of bettering their condition. It is, indeed, this inequality of condition between the front and rear ranks, in the march of progress, which gives so strong an impulse to the former to maintain their position, and to the latter to press forward into their files. This gives to progress its greatest impulse. To force the front rank back to the rear or attempt to push forward the rear into line with the front, by the interposition of the government, would put an end to the impulse and effectually arrest the march of progress.

[The "State of Nature" Purely Hypothetical]

These great and dangerous errors have their origin in the prevalent opinion that all men are born free and equal—than which nothing can be more unfounded and false. It rests upon the assumption of a fact which is contrary to universal observation, in whatever light it may be regarded. It is, indeed, difficult to explain how an opinion so destitute of all sound reason ever could have been so extensively entertained unless we regard it as being confounded with another which has some semblance of truth, but which, when properly understood, is not less false and dangerous. I refer to the assertion that all men are equal in the state of nature, meaning by a state of nature a state of individuality supposed to have existed prior

to the social and political state, and in which men lived apart
and independent of each other. If such a state ever did exist,
all men would have been, indeed, free and equal in it; that is,
free to do as they pleased and exempt from the authority or
control of others—as, by supposition, it existed anterior to
society and government. But such a state is purely hypo-
thetical. It never did nor can exist, as it is inconsistent with
the preservation and perpetuation of the race. It is, therefore,
a great misnomer to call it "the state of nature." Instead of
being the natural state of man, it is, of all conceivable states,
the most opposed to his nature—most repugnant to his feelings
and most incompatible with his wants. His natural state is
the social and political—the one for which his Creator made
him, and the only one in which he can preserve and perfect
his race. As, then, there never was such a state as the so-
called state of nature, and never can be, it follows that men,
instead of being born in it, are born in the social and political
state; and of course, instead of being born free and equal, are
born subject, not only to parental authority, but to the laws
and institutions of the country where born and under whose
protection they draw their first breath. With these remarks
I return from this digression to resume the thread of the discourse.

[CONSTITUTIONAL GOVERNMENT BETTER SUITED TO PROMOTE LIBERTY AND POWER]

It follows, from all that has been said, that the more perfectly a government combines power and liberty—that is, the
greater its power and the more enlarged and secure the liberty
of individuals—the more perfectly it fulfills the ends for which
government is ordained. To show, then, that the government
of the concurrent majority is better calculated to fulfill them
than that of the numerical, it is only necessary to explain why
the former is better suited to combine a higher degree of power
and a wider scope of liberty than the latter. I shall begin
with the former.

The concurrent majority, then, is better suited to enlarge

and secure the bounds of liberty because it is better suited to prevent government from passing beyond its proper limits and to restrict it to its primary end—the protection of the community. But in doing this, it leaves necessarily all beyond it open and free to individual exertions, and thus enlarges and secures the sphere of liberty to the greatest extent which the condition of the community will admit, as has been explained. The tendency of government to pass beyond its proper limits is what exposes liberty to danger and renders it insecure; and it is the strong counteraction of governments of the concurrent majority to this tendency which makes them so favorable to liberty. On the contrary, those of the numerical, instead of opposing and counteracting this tendency, add to it increased strength, in consequence of the violent party struggles incident to them, as has been fully explained. And hence their encroachments on liberty and the danger to which it is exposed under such governments.

So great, indeed, is the difference between the two in this respect that liberty is little more than a name under all governments of the absolute form, including that of the numerical majority, and can only have a secure and durable existence under those of the concurrent or constitutional form. The latter, by giving to each portion of the community which may be unequally affected by its action a negative on the others, prevents all partial or local legislation and restricts its action to such measures as are designed for the protection and the good of the whole. In doing this, it secures, at the same time, the rights and liberty of the people regarded individually, as each portion consists of those who, whatever may be the diversity of interests among themselves, have the same interest in reference to the action of the government.

Such being the case, the interest of each individual may be safely confided to the majority, or voice of his portion, against that of all others, and, of course, the government itself. It is only through an organism which vests each with a negative, in some one form or another, that those who have like interests in preventing the government from passing beyond its proper sphere and encroaching on the rights and liberty of individuals can cooperate peaceably and effectually in resisting the encroachments of power and thereby preserve their rights and liberty. Individual resistance is too feeble and the difficulty of concert and cooperation too great, unaided by such an organism, to oppose successfully the organized power of government with all the means of the community at its disposal, especially in populous countries of great extent where concert and cooperation are almost impossible. Even when the oppression of the government comes to be too great to be borne and force is resorted to in order to overthrow it, the result is rarely ever followed by the establishment of liberty. The force sufficient to overthrow an oppressive government is usually sufficient to establish one equally or more oppressive in its place. And hence, in no governments, except those that rest on the principle of the concurrent or constitutional majority, can the people guard their liberty against power; and hence also, when lost, the great difficulty and uncertainty of regaining it by force.

It may be further affirmed that, being more favorable to the enlargement and security of liberty, governments of the concurrent must necessarily be more favorable to progress, development, improvement, and civilization—and, of course, to the increase of power which results from and depends on these— than those of the numerical majority. That it is liberty which gives to them their greatest impulse has already been shown, and it now remains to show that these, in turn, contribute greatly to the increase of power.

In the earlier stages of society, numbers and individual prowess constituted the principal elements of power. In a more advanced stage, when communities had passed from the barbarous to the civilized state, discipline, strategy, weapons of increased power, and money—as the means of meeting increased expense—became additional and important elements. In this stage the effects of progress and improvement on the increase of power began to be disclosed, but still numbers and personal prowess were sufficient, for a long period, to enable barbarous nations to contend successfully with the civilized and, in the end, to overpower them, as the pages of history abundantly testify. But a more advanced progress, with its numerous inventions and improvements, has furnished new and far more powerful and destructive implements of offense and defense, and greatly increased the intelligence and wealth necessary to engage the skill and meet the increased expense required for their construction and application to purposes of war. The discovery of gunpowder and the use of steam as an impelling force, and their application to military purposes, have forever settled the question of ascendency between civilized and barbarous communities in favor of the former. Indeed, these, with other improvements belonging to the present state of progress, have given to communities the most advanced a superiority over those the least so, almost as great as that of the latter over the brute creation. And among the civilized, the same causes have decided the question of superiority, where other circumstances are nearly equal, in favor of those whose governments have given the greatest impulse to development, progress, and improvement; that is, to those whose liberty is the largest and best secured. Among these, England and the United States afford striking examples, not only of the effects of liberty in increasing power, but of the more perfect adaptation of governments founded on the principle of the concurrent or constitutional majority to enlarge and secure liberty. They are both governments of this description, as will be shown hereafter.

But in estimating the power of a community, moral as well as physical causes must be taken into the calculation; and in estimating the effects of liberty on power, it must not be overlooked that it is, in itself, an important agent in augmenting the force of moral as well as of physical power. It bestows on a people elevation, self-reliance, energy, and enthusiasm; and these combined give to physical power a vastly augmented and almost irresistible impetus.

These, however, are not the only elements of moral power. There are others, and among them harmony, unanimity, devotion to country, and a disposition to elevate to places of trust and power those who are distinguished for wisdom and experience. These, when the occasion requires it, will, without compulsion and from their very nature, unite and put forth the entire force of the community in the most efficient manner, without hazard to its institutions or its liberty.

All these causes combined give to a community its maximum of power. Either of them, without the other, would leave it comparatively feeble. But it cannot be necessary, after what has been stated, to enter into any further explanation or argument in order to establish the superiority of governments of the concurrent majority over the numerical in developing the great elements of moral power. So vast is this superiority that the one, by its operation, necessarily leads to their development, while the other as necessarily prevents it—as has been fully shown.

[OBJECTIONS ANSWERED]

Such are the many and striking advantages of the concurrent over the numerical majority. Against the former but two objections can be made. The one is that it is difficult of construction, which has already been sufficiently noticed; and the other that it would be impracticable to obtain the concurrence of conflicting interests where they were numerous and diversified, or, if not, that the process for this purpose would be too tardy to meet with sufficient promptness the many and dangerous emergencies to which all communities are exposed. This objection is plausible and deserves a fuller notice than it has yet received.

The diversity of opinion is usually so great on almost all questions of policy that it is not surprising, on a slight view of the subject, it should be thought impracticable to bring the various conflicting interests of a community to unite on any one line of policy, or that a government founded on such a principle would be too slow in its movements and too weak in its foundation to succeed in practice. But plausible as it may seem at the first glance, a more deliberate view will show that this opinion is erroneous. It is true that, when there is no urgent necessity, it is difficult to bring those who differ to agree on any one line of action. Each will naturally insist on taking the course he may think best, and, from pride of opinion, will be unwilling to yield to others. But the case is different when there is an urgent necessity to unite on some common course of action, as reason and experience both prove. When something *must* be done—and when it can be done only by the united consent of all—the necessity of the case will force to a compromise, be the case of that necessity what it may. On all questions of acting, necessity, where it exists, is the overruling motive; and where, in such cases, compromise among the parties is an indispensable condition to acting, it exerts an overruling influence in predisposing them to acquiesce in some one opinion or course of action. Experience furnishes many examples in confirmation of this important truth. Among these, the trial by jury is the most familiar and on that account will be selected for illustration.

In these, twelve individuals, selected without discrimination, must unanimously concur in opinion—under the obligations of an oath to find a true verdict according to law and evidence, and this, too, not unfrequently under such great difficulty and doubt that the ablest and most experienced judges and advocates differ in opinion after careful examination. And yet, as impracticable as this mode of trial would seem to a superficial observer, it is found in practice not only to succeed, but to be the safest, the wisest, and the best that human ingenuity has ever devised. When closely investigated, the cause will be found in the necessity under which the jury is placed—to agree unanimously in order to find a verdict. This necessity acts as the predisposing cause of concurrence in some common opinion, and with such efficacy that a jury rarely fails to find a verdict.

Under its potent influence, the jurors take their seats with the disposition to give a fair and impartial hearing to the arguments on both sides—meet together in the juryroom, not as disputants, but calmly to hear the opinions of each other and to compare and weigh the arguments on which they are founded, and finally to adopt that which, on the whole, is thought to be true. Under the influence of this *disposition to harmonize* one after another falls into the same opinion until unanimity is obtained. Hence its practicability—and hence also its peculiar excellence. Nothing, indeed, can be more favorable to the success of truth and justice than this predisposing influence caused by the necessity of being unanimous. It is so much so as to compensate for the defect of legal knowledge and a high degree of intelligence on the part of those who usually compose juries. If the necessity of unanimity were dispensed with and the finding of a jury made to depend on a bare majority, jury trial, instead of being one of the greatest improvements in the judicial department of government, would be one of the greatest evils that could be inflicted on the community. It would be, in such case, the conduit through which all the factious feelings of the day would enter and contaminate justice at its source.

[The Importance of Compromise]

But the same cause would act with still greater force in predisposing the various interests of the community to agree in a well-organized government founded on the concurrent majority. The necessity for unanimity, in order to keep the government in motion, would be far more urgent and would act under circumstances still more favorable to secure it. It would be superfluous, after what has been stated, to add other reasons in order to show that no necessity, physical or moral, can be more imperious than that of government. It is so much so that, to suspend its action altogether, even for an inconsiderable period, would subject the community to convulsions and anarchy. But in governments of the concurrent majority such fatal consequences can only be avoided by the unanimous concurrence or acquiesence of the various portions of the community. Such is the imperious character of the necessity which impels to compromise under governments of this description.

But to have a just conception of the overpowering influence

it would exert, the circumstances under which it would act
must be taken into consideration. These will be found, on
comparison, much more favorable than those under which
juries act. In the latter case there is nothing besides the
necessity of unanimity in finding a verdict, and the inconveni-
ence to which they might be subjected in the event of division,
to induce juries to agree except the love of truth and justice,
which, when not counteracted by some improper motive or
bias, more or less influences all, not excepting the most
depraved. In the case of governments of the concurrent
majority, there is, besides these, the love of country, than
which, if not counteracted by the unequal and oppressive
action of government or other causes, few motives exert a
greater sway. It comprehends, indeed, within itself a large
portion both of our individual and social feelings; and hence
its almost boundless control when left free to act. But the
government of the concurrent majority leaves it free by preventing abuse and oppression, and with them the whole train
of feelings and passions which lead to discord and conflict
between different portions of the community. Impelled by the
imperious necessity of preventing the suspension of the action
of government, with the fatal consequences to which it would
lead, and by the strong additional impulse derived from an
ardent love of country, each portion would regard the sacrifice
it might have to make by yielding its peculiar interest to
secure the common interest and safety of all, including its own,
as nothing compared to the evils that would be inflicted on all,
including its own, by pertinaciously adhering to a different
line of action. So powerful, indeed, would be the motives
for concurring and, under such circumstances, so weak would
be those opposed to it, the wonder would be, not that there
should, but that there should not be a compromise.

But to form a juster estimate of the full force of this impulse
to compromise, there must be added that in governments of
the concurrent majority each portion, in order to advance its
own peculiar interests, would have to conciliate all others by
showing a disposition to advance theirs; and for this purpose

each would select those to represent it whose wisdom, patriotism, and weight of character would command the confidence of the others. Under its influence—and with representatives so well qualified to accomplish the object for which they were selected—the prevailing desire would be to promote the common interests of the whole; and hence the competition would be, not which should yield the least to promote the common good, but which should yield the most. It is thus that concession would cease to be considered a sacrifice—would become a free-will offering on the altar of the country and lose the name of compromise. And herein is to be found the feature which distinguishes governments of the concurrent majority so strikingly from those of the numerical. In the latter, each faction, in the struggle to obtain the control of the government, elevates to power the designing, the artful, and unscrupulous who in their devotion to party—instead of aiming at the good of the whole—aim exclusively at securing the ascendency of party.

When traced to its source, this difference will be found to originate in the fact that in governments of the concurrent majority individual feelings are, from its organism, necessarily enlisted on the side of the social, and made to unite with them in promoting the interests of the whole as the best way of promoting the separate interests of each, while in those of the numerical majority the social are necessarily enlisted on the side of the individual and made to contribute to the interest of parties regardless of that of the whole. To effect the former—to enlist the individual on the side of the social feelings to promote the good of the whole—is the greatest possible achievement of the science of government, while to enlist the social on the side of the individual to promote the interest of parties at the expense of the good of the whole is the greatest blunder which ignorance can possibly commit.

To this also may be referred the greater solidity of foundation on which governments of the concurrent majority repose. Both ultimately rest on necessity, for force, by which those of the numerical majority are upheld, is only acquiesced in from

necessity—in a necessity not more imperious, however, than
that which compels the different portions in governments of
the concurrent majority to acquiesce in compromise. There is,
however, a great difference in the motive, the feeling, the aim
which characterize the act in the two cases. In the one, it is
done with that reluctance and hostility ever incident to
enforced submission to what is regarded as injustice and
oppression, accompanied by the desire and purpose to seize on
the first favorable opportunity for resistance; but in the other,
willingly and cheerfully, under the impulse of an exalted
patriotism, impelling all to acquiesce in whatever the common
good requires.

[The Polish Constitution]

It is, then, a great error to suppose that the government
of the concurrent majority is impracticable or that it rests on
a feeble foundation. History furnishes many examples of
such governments, and among them one in which the principle
was carried to an extreme that would be thought impracticable
had it never existed. I refer to that of Poland. In this it was
carried to such an extreme that in the election of her kings
the concurrence or acquiescence of every individual of the
nobles and gentry present, in an assembly numbering usually
from one hundred and fifty to two hundred thousand, was
required to make a choice, thus giving to each individual a
veto on his election. So, likewise, every member of her Diet
(the supreme legislative body) consisting of the king, the
senate, bishops, and deputies of the nobility and gentry of the
palatinates possessed a veto on all its proceedings—thus making a unanimous vote necessary to enact a law or to adopt any
measure whatever. And, as if to carry the principle to the
utmost extent, the veto of a single member not only defeated
the particular bill or measure in question, but prevented all
others passed during the session from taking effect. Further
the principle could not be carried. It in fact made every
individual of the nobility and gentry a distinct element in the

organism—or, to vary the expression, made him an *Estate of the kingdom*. And yet this government lasted in this form more than two centuries, embracing the period of Poland's greatest power and renown. Twice during its existence she protected Christendom, when in great danger, by defeating the Turks under the walls of Vienna and permanently arresting thereby the tide of their conquests westward.

It is true, her government was finally subverted and the people subjugated in consequence of the extreme to which the principle was carried, not, however, because of its tendency to dissolution *from weakness*, but from the facility it afforded to powerful and unscrupulous neighbors to control by their intrigues the election of her kings. But the fact that a government in which the principle was carried to the utmost extreme, not only existed, but existed for so long a period in great power and splendor, is proof conclusive both of its practicability and its compatibility with the power and permanency of government.

[The Iroquois Confederacy]

Another example, not so striking indeed, but yet deserving notice is furnished by the government of a portion of the aborigines of our own country. I refer to the Confederacy of the Six Nations who inhabited what now is called the western portion of the State of New York. One chief delegate, chosen by each nation—associated with six others of his own selection, and making in all forty-two members—constituted their federal or general government. When met, they formed the council of the union and discussed and decided all questions relating to the common welfare. As in the Polish Diet, each member possessed a veto on its decision, so that nothing could be done without the united consent of all. But this, instead of making the Confederacy weak or impracticable, had the opposite effect. It secured harmony in council and action, and with them a great increase of power. The Six Nations, in consequence, became the most powerful of all the Indian tribes within the limits of our country. They carried their conquest and authority far beyond the country they originally occupied.

I pass by, for the present, the most distinguished of all these examples—the Roman Republic, where the veto, or negative power, was carried, not indeed to the same extreme as in the Polish government, but very far and with great increase of power and stability, as I shall show more at large hereafter.

[The Free Press an Organ of Public Opinion]

It may be thought, and doubtless many have supposed, that the defects inherent in the government of the numerical majority may be remedied by a free press, as the organ of public opinion—especially in the more advanced stage of society—so as to supersede the necessity of the concurrent majority to counteract its tendency to oppression and abuse of power. It is not my aim to detract from the importance of the press, nor to underestimate the great power and influence which it has given to public opinion. On the contrary, I admit these are so great as to entitle it to be considered a new and important political element. Its influence is at the present day on the increase, and it is highly probable that it may, in combination with the causes which have contributed to raise it to its present importance, effect, in time, great changes—social and political. But however important its present influence may be or may hereafter become, or however great and beneficial the changes to which it may ultimately lead, it can never counteract the tendency of the numerical majority to the abuse of power, nor supersede the necessity of the concurrent as an essential element in the formation of constitutional governments. These it cannot effect for two reasons, either of which is conclusive.

The one is that it cannot change that principle of our nature which makes constitutions necessary to prevent government from abusing its powers, and government necessary to protect and perfect society.

Constituting, as this principle does, an essential part of our nature, no increase of knowledge and intelligence, no enlargement of our sympathetic feelings, no influence of education, or modification of the condition of society can change it. But so long as it shall continue to be an essential part of our nature, so long will government be necessary; and so long as this continues to be necessary, so long will constitutions also be necessary to counteract its tendency to the abuse of power, and so long must the concurrent majority remain an essential element in the formation of constitutions. The press may do much—by giving impulse to the progress of knowledge and intelligence—to aid the cause of education and to bring about salutary changes in the condition of society. These, in turn, may do much to explode political errors, to teach how governments should be constructed in order to fulfill their ends, and by what means they can be best preserved when so constructed. They may also do much to enlarge the social and to restrain the individual feelings, and thereby to bring about a state of things when far less power will be required by governments to guard against internal disorder and violence and external danger, and when, of course, the sphere of power may be greatly contracted and that of liberty proportionally enlarged. But all this would not change the nature of man, nor supersede the necessity of government. For so long as government exists, the possession of its control, as the means of directing its action and dispensing its honors and emoluments, will be an object of desire. While this continues to be the case, it must in governments of the numerical majority lead to party struggles and, as has been shown, to all the consequences which necessarily follow in their train, and against which the only remedy is the concurrent majority.

The other reason is to be found in the nature of the influence which the press politically exercises.

It is similar, in most respects, to that of suffrage. They are, indeed, both organs of public opinion. The principal difference is that the one has much more agency in forming public opinion, while the other gives a more authentic and authoritative expression to it. Regarded in either light, the press cannot, of itself, guard any more against the abuse of power than suffrage, and for the same reason.

If what is called public opinion were always the opinion of the whole community, the press would, as its organ, be an effective guard against the abuse of power and supersede the necessity of the concurrent majority, just as the right of suffrage would do where the community, in reference to the action of government, had but one interest. But such is not the case. On the contrary, what is called public opinion, instead of being the united opinion of the whole community, is usually nothing more than the opinion or voice of the strongest interest or combination of interests, and not unfrequently of a small but energetic and active portion of the whole. Public opinion, in relation to government and its policy, is as much divided and diversified as are the interests of the community; and the press, instead of being the organ of the whole, is usually but the organ of these various and diversified interests respectively, or rather of the parties growing out of them. It is used by them as the means of controlling public opinion and of so molding it as to promote their peculiar interests and to aid in carrying on the warfare of party. But as the organ and instrument of parties, in governments of the numerical majority, it is as incompetent as suffrage itself to counteract the tendency to oppression and abuse of power, and can no more than that supersede the necessity of the concurrent majority. On the contrary, as the instrument of party warfare, it contributes greatly to increase party excitement and the violence and virulence of party struggles, and, in the same degree, the tendency to oppression and abuse of power. Instead, then, of superseding the necessity of the concurrent majority, it increases it by increasing the violence and force of party feelings—in like manner as party caucuses and party machinery; of the latter of which, indeed, it forms an important part.

[THE STRUCTURE OF CONSTITUTIONAL AND ABSOLUTE
GOVERNMENTS]

In one respect, and only one, the government of the numerical majority has the advantage over that of the concurrent if,
indeed, it can be called an advantage. I refer to its simplicity
and facility of construction. It is simple indeed, wielded, as
it is, by a single power—the will of the greater number—and
very easy of construction. For this purpose nothing more is
necessary than universal suffrage and the regulation of the
manner of voting so as to give to the greater number the
supreme control over every department of government.

But whatever advantages simplicity and facility of construction may give it, the other forms of absolute government
possess them in a still higher degree. The construction of the
government of the numerical majority, simple as it is, requires
some preliminary measures and arrangements, while the
others, especially the monarchical, will, in its absence or where
it proves incompetent, force themselves on the community.
And hence, among other reasons, the tendency of all governments is from the more complex and difficult of construction
to the more simple and easily constructed, and, finally, to
absolute monarchy as the most simple of all. Complexity and
difficulty of construction, as far as they form objections, apply
not only to governments of the concurrent majority of the
popular form but to constitutional governments of every form.
The least complex and the most easily constructed of them are
much more complex and difficult of construction than any one
of the absolute forms. Indeed, so great has been this difficulty
that their construction has been the result, not so much of
wisdom and patriotism, as of favorable combinations of circumstances. They have for the most part grown out of the
struggles between conflicting interests which, from some fortunate turn, have ended in a compromise by which both parties
have been admitted, in some one way or another, to have a
separate and distinct voice in the government. Where this has

not been the case, they have been the product of fortunate circumstances acting in conjunction with some pressing danger which forced their adoption as the only means by which it could be avoided. It would seem that it has exceeded human sagacity deliberately to plan and construct constitutional governments, with a full knowledge of the principles on which they were formed, or to reduce them to practice without the pressure of some immediate and urgent necessity. Nor is it surprising that such should be the case, for it would seem almost impossible for any man, or body of men, to be so profoundly and thoroughly acquainted with the people of any community which has made any considerable progress in civilization and wealth, with all the diversified interests ever accompanying them, as to be able to organize constitutional governments suited to their condition. But even were this possible, it would be difficult to find any community sufficiently enlightened and patriotic to adopt such a government without the compulsion of some pressing necessity. A constitution, to succeed, must spring from the bosom of the community and be adapted to the intelligence and character of the people and all the multifarious relations, internal and external, which distinguish one people from another. If it does not, it will prove in practice to be not a constitution, but a cumbrous and useless machine which must be speedily superseded and laid aside for some other more simple and better suited to their condition.

It would thus seem almost necessary that governments should commence in some one of the simple and absolute forms which, however well suited to the community in its earlier stages, must in its progress lead to oppression and abuse of power and finally to an appeal to force—to be succeeded by a military despotism—unless the conflicts to which it leads should be fortunately adjusted by a compromise which will give to the respective parties a participation in the control of the government, and thereby lay the foundation of a constitutional government to be afterwards matured and perfected. Such governments have been, emphatically, the product of circumstances. And hence the difficulty of one people imitating the government of another. And hence also the importance of terminating all civil conflicts by a compromise which shall prevent either party from obtaining complete control and thus subjecting the other.

[POPULAR GOVERNMENT]

Of the different forms of constitutional governments, the popular is the most complex and difficult of construction. It is, indeed, so difficult that ours, it is believed, may with truth be said to be the only one of a purely popular character, of any considerable importance, that ever existed. The cause is to be found in the fact that in the other two forms society is arranged in artificial orders or classes. Where these exist the line of distinction between them is so strongly marked as to throw into shade or, otherwise, to absorb all interests which are foreign to them respectively. Hence in an aristocracy all interests are, politically, reduced to two—the nobles and the people; and in a monarchy with a nobility into three—the monarch, the nobles, and the people. In either case they are so few that the sense of each may be taken separately through its appropriate organ so as to give to each a concurrent voice, and a negative on the other, through the usual departments of the government, without making it too complex or too tardy in its movements to perform with promptness and energy all the necessary functions of government.

The case is different in constitutional governments of the popular form. In consequence of the absence of these artificial distinctions the various natural interests, resulting from diversity of pursuits, condition, situation, and character of different portions of the people—and from the action of the government itself—rise into prominence and struggle to obtain the ascendency. They will, it is true, in governments of the numerical majority ultimately coalesce and form two great parties, but not so closely as to lose entirely their separate character and existence. These they will ever be ready to reassume when the objects for which they coalesced are accomplished. To overcome the difficulties occasioned by so great a diversity of interests, an organism far more complex is necessary.

Another obstacle, difficult to be overcome, opposes the formation of popular constitutional governments. It is much more difficult to terminate the struggles between conflicting interests by compromise in absolute popular governments than in an aristocracy or monarchy.

[ARISTOCRACY]

In an aristocracy the object of the people in the ordinary struggle between them and the nobles is not, at least in its early stages, to overthrow the nobility and revolutionize the government, but to participate in its powers. Notwithstanding the oppression to which they may be subjected under this form of government, the people commonly feel no small degree of respect for the descendants of a long line of distinguished ancestors, and do not usually aspire to more—in opposing the authority of the nobles—than to obtain such a participation in the powers of the government as will enable them to correct its abuses and to lighten their burdens. Among the nobility, on the other hand, it sometimes happens that there are individuals of great influence with both sides who have the good sense and patriotism to interpose in order to effect a compromise by yielding to the reasonable demands of the people, and thereby to avoid the hazard of a final and decisive appeal to force. It is thus by a judicious and timely compromise the people in such governments may be raised to a participation in the administration sufficient for their protection without the loss of authority on the part of the nobles.

[MONARCHY]

In the case of a monarchy, the process is somewhat different. Where it is a military despotism, the people rarely have the spirit or intelligence to attempt resistance, or, if otherwise, their resistance must almost necessarily terminate in defeat or in a mere change of dynasty—by the elevation of their leader to the throne. It is different where the monarch is surrounded by an hereditary nobility. In a struggle between him and them, both (but especially the monarch) are usually disposed to court the people in order to enlist them on their respective sides—a state of things highly favorable to their elevation. In this case the struggle, if it should be long continued without decisive results, would almost necessarily raise them to political importance and to a participation in the powers of the government.

[ABSOLUTE DEMOCRACY]

The case is different in an absolute democracy. Party conflicts between the majority and minority in such governments can hardly ever terminate in compromise. The object of the opposing minority is to expel the majority from power, and of the majority to maintain their hold upon it. It is on both sides a struggle for the whole—a struggle that must determine which shall be the governing and which the subject party—and in character, object, and result not unlike that between competitors for the scepter in absolute monarchies. Its regular course, as has been shown, is excessive violence—an appeal to force—followed by revolution and terminating at last in the elevation to supreme power of the general of the successful party. And hence, among other reasons, aristocracies and monarchies more readily assume the constitutional form than absolute popular governments.

Of the three different forms, the monarchical has heretofore been much the most prevalent and generally the most powerful and durable. This result is doubtless to be attributed principally to the fact that in its absolute form it is the most simple and easily constructed. And hence, as government is indispensable, communities, having too little intelligence to form or preserve the others, naturally fall into this. It may also in part be attributed to another cause already alluded to —that in its organism and character it is much more closely assimilated than either of the other two to military power, on which all absolute governments depend for support. And hence also the tendency of the others and of constitutional governments which have been so badly constructed or become so disorganized as to require force to support them—to pass into military despotism, that is, into monarchy in its most absolute and simple form. And hence again the fact that revolutions in absolute monarchies end almost invariably in a change of dynasty, and not of the forms of the government, as is almost universally the case in the other systems.

But there are, besides these, other causes of a higher character which contribute much to make monarchies the most prevalent and usually the most durable governments. Among them the leading one is, they are the most susceptible of improvement—that is, they can be more easily and readily modified so as to prevent, to a limited extent, oppression and abuse of power without assuming the constitutional form in its strict sense. It slides, almost naturally, into one of the most important modifications. I refer to hereditary descent. When this becomes well defined and firmly established, the community or kingdom comes to be regarded by the sovereign as the hereditary possession of his family—a circumstance which tends strongly to identify his interests with those of his subjects and thereby to mitigate the rigor of the government. It gives, besides, great additional security to his person and prevents, in the same degree, not only the suspicion and hostile feelings incident to insecurity, but invites all those kindly feelings which naturally spring up on both sides between those whose interests are identified, when there is nothing to prevent it. And hence the strong feelings of paternity on the side of the sovereign and of loyalty on that of his subjects, which are often exhibited in such governments.

There is another improvement of which it is readily susceptible, nearly allied to the preceding. The hereditary principle not unfrequently extends to other families—especially to those of the distinguished chieftains by whose aid the monarchy was established, when it originates in conquest. When this is the case and a powerful body of hereditary nobles surround the sovereign, they oppose a strong resistance to his authority, and he to theirs—tending to the advantage and security of the people. Even when they do not succeed in obtaining a participation in the powers of the government, they usually acquire sufficient weight to be felt and respected. From this state of things such governments usually, in time, settle down on some fixed rules of action which the sovereign is compelled to respect and by which increased protection and security are acquired by all. It was thus the enlightened monarchies of Europe were formed under which the people of that portion of the globe have made such great advances in power, intelligence, and civilization.

To these may be added the greater capacity which governments of the monarchical form have exhibited to hold under subjection a large extent of territory and a numerous population, and which has made them more powerful than others of a different form to the extent that these constitute an element of power. All these causes combined have given such great and decisive advantages as to enable them heretofore to absorb, in the progress of events, the few governments which have from time to time assumed different forms—not excepting even the mighty Roman Republic, which, after attaining the highest point of power, passed, seemingly under the operation of irresistible causes, into a military despotism. I say heretofore—for it remains to be seen whether they will continue to retain their advantages in these respects over the others under the great and growing influence of public opinion and the new and imposing form which popular government has assumed with us.

These have already effected great changes and will probably effect still greater—adverse to the monarchical form; but as yet these changes have tended rather to the absolute than to the constitutional form of popular government—for reasons which have been explained. If this tendency should continue permanently in the same direction, the monarchical form must still retain its advantages and continue to be the most prevalent. Should this be the case, the alternative will be between monarchy and popular government in the form of the numerical majority—or absolute democracy; which, as has been shown, is not only the most fugitive of all the forms, but has the strongest tendency of all others to the monarchical. If, on the contrary, this tendency, or the changes referred to, should incline to the constitutional form of popular government—and a proper organism come to be regarded as not less indispensable than the right of suffrage to the establishment of such governments—in such case it is not improbable that in the progress of events the monarchical will cease to be the prevalent form of government. Whether they will take this direction, at least for a long time will depend on the success of our government and a correct understanding of the principles on which it is constructed.

[THE ROLE OF PUBLIC OPINION]

To comprehend more fully the force and bearing of public opinion and to form a just estimate of the changes to which, aided by the press, it will probably lead, politically and socially—it will be necessary to consider it in connection with the causes that have given it an influence so great as to entitle it to be regarded as a new political element. They will upon investigation be found in the many discoveries and inventions made in the last few centuries.

Among the more prominent of those of an earlier date stand the practical application of the magnetic power to the purposes of navigation by the invention of the mariner's compass, the discovery of the mode of making gunpowder and its application to the art of war, and the invention of the art of printing. Among the more recent are the numerous chemical and mechanical discoveries and inventions and their application to the various arts of production, the application of steam to machinery of almost every description, especially to such as is designed to facilitate transportation and travel by land and water, and finally the invention of the magnetic telegraph.

All these have led to important results. Through the invention of the mariner's compass the globe has been circumnavigated and explored, and all who inhabit it, with but few exceptions, brought within the sphere of an all-pervading commerce, which is daily diffusing over its surface the light and blessings of civilization. Through that of the art of printing the fruits of observation and reflection, of discoveries and inventions, with all the accumulated stores of previously acquired knowledge, are preserved and widely diffused. The application of gunpowder to the art of war has forever settled the long conflict for ascendency between civilization and barbarism in favor of the former, and thereby guarantied that whatever knowledge is now accumulated or may hereafter be added shall never again be lost. The numerous discoveries and inventions, chemical and mechanical, and the application of steam to machinery have increased many-fold the productive powers of labor and capital, and have thereby greatly increased the number who may devote themselves to study and improvement—and the amount of means necessary for commercial exchanges, especially between the more and the less advanced and civilized portions of the globe, to the great advantage of both, but particularly of the latter. The application of steam to the purposes of travel and transportation by land and water has vastly increased the facility, cheapness and rapidity of both—diffusing with them information and intelligence almost as quickly and as freely as if borne by the winds, while the electrical wires outstrip them in velocity, rivalling in rapidity even thought itself.

The joint effect of all has been a great increase and diffusion of knowledge, and with this an impulse to progress and civilization heretofore unexampled in the history of the world—accompanied by a mental energy and activity unprecedented.

To all these causes public opinion and its organ, the press, owe their origin and great influence. Already they have attained a force in the more civilized portions of the globe sufficient to be felt by all governments, even the most absolute and despotic. But as great as they now are, they have as yet attained nothing like their maximum force. It is probable that not one of the causes which have contributed to their formation and influence has yet produced its full effect, while several of the most powerful have just begun to operate; and many others, probably of equal or even greater force, yet remain to be brought to light.

When the causes now in operation have produced their full effect and inventions and discoveries shall have been exhausted —if that may ever be, they will give a force to public opinion and cause changes, political and social, difficult to be anticipated. What will be their final bearing, time only can decide with any certainty. That they will, however, greatly improve the condition of man ultimately, it would be impious to doubt. It would be to suppose that the all-wise and beneficient Being, the Creator of all, had so constituted man as that the employment of the high intellectual faculties with which He has been pleased to endow him—in order that he might develop the laws that control the great agents of the material world and make them subservient to his use—would prove to him the cause of permanent evil, and not of permanent good. If, then, such a supposition be inadmissable, they must, in their orderly and full development, end in his permanent good. But this cannot be unless the ultimate effect of their action, politically, shall be to give ascendency to that form of government best calculated to fulfill the ends for which government is ordained. For so completely does the well-being of our race depend on good government that it is hardly possible any change the ultimate effect of which should be otherwise could prove to be a permanent good.

It is, however, not improbable that many and great, but temporary evils will follow the changes they have effected and are destined to effect. It seems to be a law in the political as well as in the material world that great changes cannot be made, except very gradually, without convulsions and revolutions—to be followed by calamities in the beginning, however beneficial they may prove to be in the end. The first effect of such changes on long-established governments will be to unsettle the opinions and principles in which they originated and which have guided their policy before those which the changes are calculated to form and establish are fairly developed and understood. The interval between the decay of the old and the formation and establishment of the new constitutes a period of transition which must always necessarily be one of uncertainty, confusion, error, and wild and fierce fanaticism.

The governments of the more advanced and civilized portions of the world are now in the midst of this period. It has proved and will continue to prove a severe trial to existing political institutions of every form. Those governments which have not the sagacity to perceive what is truly public opinion —to distinguish between it and the mere clamor of faction, or shouts of fanaticism—and the good sense and firmness to yield timely and cautiously to the claims of the one, and to resist promptly and decidedly the demands of the other, are doomed to fall. Few will be able successfully to pass through this period of transition; and these not without shocks and modifications more or less considerable. It will endure until the governing and the governed shall better understand the ends for which government is ordained, and the form best adapted to accomplish them under all the circumstances in which communities may be respectively placed.

I shall, in conclusion, proceed to exemplify the elementary principles which have been established by giving a brief account of the origin and character of the governments of Rome and Great Britain, the two most remarkable and perfect of their respective forms of constitutional governments. The object is to show how these principles were applied in the more simple forms of such governments, preparatory to an exposition of the mode in which they have been applied in our own more complex system. It will appear that in each the principles are the same, and that the difference in their application resulted from the different situation and social condition of the respective communities. They were modified in each so as to conform to these; and hence their remarkable success. They were applied to communities in which hereditary rank had long prevailed. Their respective constitutions originated in concession to the people; and through them they acquired a participation in the powers of government. But with us they were applied to communities where all political rank and distinction between citizens were excluded and where government had its origin in the will of the people.

But however different their origin and character, it will be found that the object in each was the same—to blend and harmonize the conflicting interests of the community; and the means the same—taking the sense of each class or portion through its appropriate organ and considering the concurrent sense of all as the sense of the whole community. Such being the fact, an accurate and clear conception how this was effected in their more simple forms will enable us better to understand how it was accomplished in our far more refined, artificial, and complex form.

[THE ROMAN CONSTITUTION]

It is well known to all, the least conversant with their history, that the Roman people consisted of two distinct orders or classes—the Patricians and the Plebeians; and that the line of distinction was so strongly drawn that for a long time the right of intermarriage between them was prohibited. After the overthrow of the monarchy and the expulsion of the Tarquins, the government fell exclusively under the control of the patricians, who, with their clients and dependents, formed, at the time, a very numerous and powerful body. At first, while there was danger of the return of the exiled family, they treated the plebeians with kindness, but after it had passed away, with oppression and cruelty.

It is not necessary, with the object in view, to enter into a minute account of the various acts of oppression and cruelty to which they were subjected. It is sufficient to state that, according to the usages of war at the time, the territory of a conquered people became the property of the conquerors, and that the plebeians were harassed and oppressed by incessant wars in which the danger and toil were theirs, while all the fruits of victory (the lands of the vanquished, and the spoils of war) accrued to the benefit of their oppressors. The result was such as might be expected. They were impoverished and forced, from necessity, to borrow from the patricians at usurious and exorbitant interest funds with which they had been enriched through their blood and toil, and to pledge their all for repayment at stipulated periods. In case of default the pledge became forfeited; and under the provisions of law in such cases the debtors were liable to be seized and sold or imprisoned by their creditors in private jails prepared and kept for the purpose. These savage provisions were enforced with the utmost rigor against the indebted and impoverished plebeians. They constituted, indeed, an essential part of the system through which they were plundered and oppressed by the patricians.

A system so oppressive could not be endured. The natural consequences followed. Deep hatred was engendered between the orders, accompanied by factions, violence, and corruption, which distracted and weakened the government. At length, an incident occurred which roused the indignation of the plebeians to the utmost pitch and which ended in an open rupture between the two orders.

An old soldier who had long served the country and had fought with bravery in twenty-eight battles made his escape from the prison of his creditor—squalid, pale, and famished. He implored the protection of the plebeians. A crowd surrounded him, and his tale of service to the country and the cruelty with which he had been treated by his creditor kindled a flame which continued to rage until it extended to the army. It refused to continue any longer in service—crossed the Anio and took possession of the sacred mount. The patricians divided in opinion as to the course which should be pursued. The more violent insisted on an appeal to arms, but fortunately the counsel of the moderate which recommended concession and compromise prevailed. Commissioners were appointed to treat with the army, and a formal compact was entered into between the orders and ratified by the oaths of each which conceded to the plebeians the right to elect two

tribunes as the protectors of their order, and made their
persons sacred. The number was afterwards increased to ten,
and their election by centuries changed to election by tribes
—a mode by which the plebeians secured a decided
preponderance.

Such was the origin of the tribunate which in process of
time opened all the honors of the government to the plebeians.
They acquired the right, not only of vetoing the passage of
all laws, but also their execution, and thus obtained through
their tribunes a negative on the entire action of the government without divesting the patricians of their control over
the Senate. By this arrangement the government was placed
under the concurrent and joint voice of the two orders
expressed through separate and appropriate organs—the one
possessing the positive, and the other the negative powers of
the government. This simple change converted it from an
absolute into a constitutional government—from a government of the patricians only to that of the whole Roman people
and from an aristocracy into a republic. In doing this, it laid
the solid foundation of Roman liberty and greatness.

A superficial observer would pronounce a government so
organized as that one order should have the power of making
and executing the laws, and another, or the representatives of
another, the unlimited authority of preventing their enactment
and execution—if not wholly impracticable, at least too feeble
to stand the shocks to which all governments are subject, and
would therefore predict its speedy dissolution after a distracted and inglorious career.

How different from the result! Instead of distraction, it
proved to be the bond of concord and harmony; instead of
weakness, of unequaled strength; and, instead of a short and
inglorious career, one of great length and immortal glory. It
moderated the conflicts between the orders, harmonized their
interests and blended them into one, substituted devotion to
country in the place of devotion to particular orders, called
forth the united strength and energy of the whole in the hour
of danger, raised to power the wise and patriotic, elevated the

Roman name above all others, extended her authority and
dominion over the greater part of the then known world and
transmitted the influence of her laws and institutions to the
present day. Had the opposite counsel prevailed at this criti-
cal juncture, had an appeal been made to arms instead of to
concession and compromise, Rome, instead of being what she
afterward became, would in all probability have been as
inglorious and as little known to posterity as the insignificant
states which surrounded her, whose names and existence would
have been long since consigned to oblivion had they not been
preserved in the history of her conquests of them. But for
the wise course then adopted, it is not improbable—whichever
order might have prevailed—that she would have fallen under
some cruel and petty tyrant and finally been conquered by
some of the neighboring states or by the Carthaginians or the
Gauls. To the fortunate turn which events then took she
owed her unbounded sway and imperishable renown.

It is true that the tribunate, after raising her to a height of
power and prosperity never before equaled, finally became one
of the instruments by which her liberty was overthrown; but
it was not until she became exposed to new dangers growing
out of increase of wealth and the great extent of her dominions,
against which the tribunate furnished no guards. Its original
object was the protection of the plebeians against oppression
and abuse of power on the part of the patricians. This it thoroughly accomplished, but it had no power to protect the people
of the numerous and wealthy conquered countries from being
plundered by consuls and proconsuls. Nor could it prevent
the plunderers from using the enormous wealth which they
extorted from the impoverished and ruined provinces to corrupt and debase the people, nor arrest the formation of parties
(irrespective of the old division of patricians and plebeians)
having no other object than to obtain the control of the
government for the purpose of plunder. Against these formidable evils her constitution furnished no adequate security.
Under their baneful influence the possession of the government
became the object of the most violent conflicts, not between

patricians and plebeians, but between profligate and corrupt factions. They continued with increasing violence until finally Rome sunk, as must every community under similar circumstances, beneath the strong grasp, the despotic rule of the chieftain of the successful party—the sad but only alternative which remained to prevent universal violence, confusion, and anarchy. The Republic had in reality ceased to exist long before the establishment of the Empire. The interval was filled by the rule of ferocious, corrupt, and bloody factions. There was, indeed, a small but patriotic body of eminent individuals who struggled in vain to correct abuses and to restore the government to its primitive character and purity, and who sacrificed their lives in their endeavors to accomplish an object so virtuous and noble. But it can be no disparagement to the tribunate that the great powers conferred on it for wise purposes, and which it had so fully accomplished, should be seized upon during this violent and corrupt interval to overthrow the liberty it had established and so long nourished and supported.

In assigning such consequence to the tribunate I must not overlook other important provisions of the constitution of the Roman government. The Senate, as far as we are informed, seems to have been admirably constituted to secure consistency and steadiness of action. The power—when the Republic was exposed to imminent danger—to appoint a dictator vested for a limited period with almost boundless authority, the two consuls and the manner of electing them, the auguries, the sibylline books, the priesthood, and the censorship—all of which appertained to the patricians—were perhaps indispensable to withstand the vast and apparently irregular power of the tribunate, while the possession of such great powers by the patricians made it necessary to give proportionate strength to the only organ through which the plebeians could act on the government with effect. The government was, indeed, powerfully constituted and apparently well proportioned both in its positive and negative organs. It was truly an iron government. Without the tribunate it proved to be one of the most oppressive and cruel that ever existed, but with it, one of the strongest and best.

[THE BRITISH CONSTITUTION]

The origin and character of the British government are so well known that a very brief sketch, with the object in view, will suffice.

The causes which ultimately molded it into its present form commenced with the Norman Conquest. This introduced the feudal system with its necessary appendages—a hereditary monarchy and nobility; the former in the line of the chief who led the invading army, and the latter in that of his distinguished followers. They became his feudatories. The country—both land and people (the latter as serfs)—was divided between them. Conflicts soon followed between the monarch and the nobles—as must ever be the case under such systems. They were followed, in the progress of events, by efforts on the part both of monarchs and nobles to conciliate the favor of the people. They, in consequence, gradually rose to power. At every step of their ascent they became more important—and were more and more courted—until at length their influence was so sensibly felt that they were summoned to attend the meeting of the parliament by delegates, not, however, as an estate of the realm or constituent member of the body politic. The first summons came from the nobles, and was designed to conciliate their good feelings and secure their cooperation in the war against the king. This was followed by one from him, but his object was simply to have them present at the meeting of parliament in order to be *consulted* by the crown on questions relating to taxes and supplies, not, indeed, to discuss the right to lay the one and to raise the other—for the king claimed the arbitrary authority to do both —but with a view to facilitate their collection and to reconcile them to their imposition.

From this humble beginning, they, after a long struggle, accompanied by many vicissitudes, raised themselves to be considered one of the estates of the realm, and finally in their efforts to enlarge and secure what they had gained overpowered, for a time, the other two estates and thus concentrated all power in a single estate or body. This, in effect, made the government absolute and led to consequences which, as by a fixed law, must ever result in popular governments of this form—namely, to organized parties, or rather factions, contending violently to obtain or retain the control of the government; and this again, by laws almost as uniform, to the concentration of all the powers of government in the hands of the military commander of the successful party.

His heir was too feeble to hold the scepter he had grasped, and the general discontent with the result of the revolution led to the restoration of the old dynasty without defining the limits between the powers of the respective estates.

After a short interval, another revolution followed in which the lords and commons united against the king. This terminated in his overthrow and the transfer of the crown to a collateral branch of the family, accompanied by a declaration of rights which defined the powers of the several estates of the realm, and finally perfected and established the constitution. Thus a feudal monarchy was converted, through a slow but steady process of many centuries, into a highly refined constitutional monarchy without changing the basis of the original government.

As it now stands, the realm consists of three estates: the king, the lords temporal and spiritual, and the commons. The parliament is the grand council. It possesses the supreme power. It enacts laws by the concurring assent of the lords and commons—subject to the approval of the king. The executive power is vested in the monarch, who is regarded as constituting the first estate. Although irresponsible himself, he can only act through responsible ministers and agents. They are responsible to the other estates—to the lords as constituting the high court before whom all the servants of the crown may be tried for malpractices and crimes against the realm or official delinquencies and to the commons as possessing the impeaching power and constituting the grand inquest of the kingdom. These provisions, with their legislative powers —especially that of withholding supplies—give them a controlling influence on the executive department and virtually a participation in its power—so that the acts of the government, throughout its entire range, may be fairly considered as the result of the concurrent and joint action of the three estates— and, as these embrace all the orders, of concurrent and joint action of the estates of the realm.

He would take an imperfect and false view of the subject who should consider the king in his mere individual character, or even as the head of the royal family—as constituting an estate. Regarded in either light, so far from deserving to be considered as the First Estate and the head of the realm, as he is, he would represent an interest too inconsiderable to be an object of special protection. Instead of this, he represents what in reality is habitually and naturally the most powerful interest, all things considered, under every form of government in all civilized communities—*the tax-consuming interest* or, more broadly, the great interest which necessarily grows out of the action of the government, be its form what it may—the interest that *lives by the government.* It is composed of the recipients of its honors and emoluments and may be properly called the government interest or party—in contradistinction to the rest of the community, or (as they may be properly called) the people or commons. The one comprehends all who are supported by the government, and the other all who support the government; and it is only because the former are strongest, all things being considered, that they are enabled to retain for any considerable time advantages so great and commanding.

This great and predominant interest is naturally represented by a single head. For it is impossible, without being so represented, to distribute the honors and emoluments of the government among those who compose it without producing discord and conflict; and it is only by preventing these that advantages so tempting can be long retained. And hence the strong tendency of this great interest to the monarchical form—that is, to be represented by a single individual. On the contrary, the antagonistic interest, that which supports the government, has the opposite tendency—a tendency to be represented by many, because a large assembly can better judge than one individual or a few what burdens the community can bear and how it can be most equally distributed and easily collected.

In the British government, the king constitutes an Estate, because he is the head and representative of this great interest. He is the conduit through which all the honors and emoluments of the government flow, while the House of Commons, according to the theory of the government, is the head and representative of the opposite—the great taxpaying interest by which the government is supported.

Between these great interests there is necessarily a constant and strong tendency to conflict, which, if not counteracted, must end in violence and an appeal to force, to be followed by revolution, as has been explained. To prevent this the House of Lords, as one of the Estates of the realm, is interposed and constitutes the conservative power of the government. It consists, in fact, of that portion of the community who are the principal recipients of the honors, emoluments, and other advantages derived from the government, and whose condition cannot be improved, but must be made worse by the triumph of either of the conflicting Estates over the other; and hence it is opposed to the ascendency of either and in favor of preserving the equilibrium between them.

This sketch, brief as it is, is sufficient to show that these two constitutional governments—by far the most illustrious of their respective kinds—conform to the principles that have been established, alike in their origin and in their construction. The constitutions of both originated in a pressure occasioned by conflicts of interests between hostile classes or orders and were intended to meet the pressing exigencies of the occasion, neither party, it would seem, having any conception of the principles involved or the consequences to follow beyond the immediate objects in contemplation. It would, indeed, seem almost impossible for constitutional governments founded on orders or classes to originate in any other manner. It is difficult to conceive that any people among whom they did not exist would or could voluntarily institute them in order to establish such governments, while it is not at all wonderful that they should grow out of conflicts between different orders or classes when aided by a favorable combination of circumstances.

The constitutions of both rest on the same principle—an organism by which the voice of each order or class is taken through its appropriate organ, and which requires the concurring voice of all to constitute that of the whole community. The effects, too, were the same in both—to unite and harmonize conflicting interests, to strengthen attachments to the whole community and to moderate that to the respective orders or classes, to rally all in the hour of danger around the standard of their country, to elevate the feeling of nationality, and to develop power, moral and physical, to an extraordinary extent. Yet each has its distinguishing features resulting from the difference of their organisms and the circumstances in which they respectively originated.

In the government of Great Britain, the three orders are blended in the legislative department, so that the separate and concurring act of each is necessary to make laws, while, on the contrary, in the Roman, one order had the power of making laws, and another of annulling them or arresting their execution. Each had its peculiar advantages. The Roman developed more fully the love of country and the feelings of nationality. "I am a Roman citizen," was pronounced with a pride and elevation of sentiment never, perhaps, felt before or since by any citizen or subject of any community in announcing the country to which he belonged.

It also developed more fully the power of the community. Taking into consideration their respective population and the state of the arts at the different periods, Rome developed more power, comparatively, than Great Britain ever has—vast as that is and has been—or, perhaps, than any other community ever did. Hence the mighty control she acquired from a beginning so humble. But the British government is far superior to that of Rome in its adaptation and capacity to embrace under its control extensive dominions without subverting its constitution. In this respect, the Roman constitution was defective and, in consequence, soon began to exhibit marks of decay, after Rome had extended her dominions beyond Italy, while the British holds under its sway, without apparently impairing either, an empire equal to that under the weight of which the constitution and liberty of Rome were crushed. The great advantage it derives from its different structure, especially that of the executive department, and the character of its conservative principle. The former is so constructed as to prevent, in consequence of its unity and hereditary character, the violent and factious struggles to obtain the control of the government—and, with it, the vast patronage which distracted, corrupted, and finally subverted the Roman Republic. Against this fatal disease the latter had no security whatever, while the British government—besides the advantages it possesses, in this respect, from the structure of its executive department—has in the character of its conservative principle another and powerful security against it. Its character is such that patronage, instead of weakening, strengthens it. For the greater the patronage of the government, the greater will be the share which falls to the estate constituting the conservative department of the government; and the more eligible its condition, the greater its opposition to any radical change in its form. The two causes combined give to the government a greater capacity of holding under subjection extensive dominions without subverting the constitution or destroying liberty than has ever been possessed by any other. It is difficult, indeed, to assign any limit to its capacity in this respect. The most probable which can be assigned is its ability to bear increased burdens; the taxation necessary to meet the expenses incident to the acquisition and government of such vast dominions may prove in the end so heavy as to crush under its weight the laboring and productive portions of the population.

I have now finished the brief sketch I proposed of the origin and character of these two renowned governments and shall next proceed to consider the character, origin, and structure of the Government of the United States. It differs from the Roman and British more than they differ from each other; and although an existing government of recent origin, its character and structure are perhaps less understood than those of either.

A DISCOURSE ON THE CONSTITUTION AND GOVERNMENT OF THE UNITED STATES

[Selections]

A DISCOURSE ON THE CONSTITUTION AND GOVERNMENT OF THE UNITED STATES

[FORMATION OF THE FEDERAL REPUBLIC][1]

Ours is a system of governments, compounded of the separate governments of the several States composing the Union and of one common government of all its members, called the Government of the United States. The former preceded the latter, which was created by their agency. Each was framed by written constitutions; those of the several States by the people of each, acting separately and in their sovereign character; and that of the United States by the same, acting in the same character, but jointly instead of separately. All were formed on the same model. They all divide the powers of government into legislative, executive, and judicial; and are founded on the great principle of the responsibility of the rulers to the ruled. The entire powers of government are divided between the two, those of a more general character being specifically delegated to the United States, and all others not delegated being reserved to the several States in their separate character. Each, within its appropriate sphere, possesses all the attributes and performs all the functions of government. Neither is perfect without the other. The two combined form one entire and perfect government. With these preliminary remarks, I shall proceed to the consideration of the immediate subject of this discourse.

The Government of the United States was formed by the Constitution of the United States, and ours is a democratic, federal republic.

[1] From *The Works of John C. Calhoun*, edited by Richard K. Crallé (New York, 1853), Vol. I, pp. 111-131.

It is democratic, in contradistinction to aristocracy and monarchy. It excludes classes, orders, and all artificial distinctions. To guard against their introduction, the constitution prohibits the granting of any title of nobility by the United States or by any State.[2] The whole system is indeed democratic throughout. It has for its fundamental principle the great cardinal maxim that the people are the source of all power; that the governments of the several States and of the United States were created by them and for them; that the powers conferred on them are not surrendered but delegated, and as such are held in trust and not absolutely, and can be rightfully exercised only in furtherance of the objects for which they were delegated.

It is federal as well as democratic. *Federal*, on the one hand, in contradistinction to *national*; and, on the other, to a *confederacy*. In showing this, I shall begin with the former.

It is federal because it is the government of States united in a political union, in contradistinction to a government of individuals socially united, that is, by what is usually called a social compact. To express it more concisely, it is federal and not national because it is the government of a community of States, and not the government of a single State or nation.

That it is federal and not national we have the high authority of the Convention which framed it. General Washington, as its organ, in his letter submitting the plan to the consideration of the Congress of the then Confederacy, calls it in one place "the general government of the Union" and in another "the federal government of these States." Taken together, the plain meaning is that the government proposed would be, if adopted, the government of the States adopting it, in their united character as members of a common Union, and as such would be a federal government. These expressions were not used without due consideration and an accurate and full knowledge of their true import. The subject was not a novel one. The Convention was familiar with it. It was

[2] 1st Art. 9 and 10 Sec.—*Author*.

much agitated in their deliberations. They divided in reference to it in the early stages of their proceedings. At first one party was in favor of a national and the other of a federal government. The former, in the beginning, prevailed; and in the plans which they proposed the Constitution and government are styled "national." But finally the latter gained the ascendency, when the term "national" was superseded and "United States" substituted in its place. The Constitution was accordingly styled "the Constitution of the United States of America," and the government "the Government of the United States," leaving out "America" for the sake of brevity. It cannot admit of a doubt that the Convention, by the expression "United States," meant the States united in a federal Union; for in no other sense could they, with propriety, call the government "the federal government of these States" and "the general government of the Union," as they did in the letter referred to. It is thus clear that the Convention regarded the different expression, "the federal government of the United States," as meaning the same thing—a federal, in contradistinction to a national, government.

Assuming it then as established that they are the same, it is only necessary in order to ascertain with precision what they meant by "federal government" to ascertain what they meant by "the Government of the United States." For this purpose it will be necessary to trace the expression to its origin.

It was at that time, as our history shows, an old and familiar phrase, having a known and well-defined meaning. Its use commenced with the political birth of these States; and it has been applied to them, in all the forms of government through which they have passed, without alteration. The style of the present Constitution and government is precisely the style by which the Confederacy that existed when it was adopted and which it superseded was designated. The instrument that formed the latter was called "Articles of Confederation and Perpetual Union." Its first Article declares that the style of this Confederacy shall be "The United States of America"; and the second, in order to leave no doubt as to the relation in which the States should stand to each other in the Confederacy about to be formed, declared: "Each State retains its sovereignty, freedom and independence; and every power, jurisdiction, and right which is not, by this confederation, expressly delegated to the United States in Congress assembled." If we go one step further back, the style of the Confederacy will be found to be the same with that of the Revolutionary government which existed when it was adopted and which it superseded. It dates its origin with the Declaration of Independence. That act is styled "The unanimous Declaration of the thirteen United States of America." And here again, that there might be no doubt how these States would stand to each other in the new condition in which they were about to be placed, it concluded by declaring "that these United Colonies are, and of right ought to be, free and independent States," "and that, as free and independent States, they have full power to levy war, conclude peace, contract alliances, and to do all other acts and things which independent States may of right do." The "United States" is, then, the baptismal name of these States, received at their birth, by which they have ever since continued to call themselves, by which they have characterized their constitution, government, and laws; and by which they are known to the rest of the world.

The retention of the same style throughout every stage of their existence affords strong, if not conclusive, evidence that the political relation between these States, under their present Constitution and government, is substantially the same as under the Confederacy and Revolutionary government; and what that relation was we are not left to doubt, as they are declared expressly to be "*free, independent, and sovereign* States." They, then, are now united, and have been throughout, simply as confederated States. If it had been intended by the members of the Convention which framed the present Constitution and government to make any essential change, either in the relation of the States to each other or the basis of their union, they would, by retaining the style which designated them under the preceding governments, have practiced a deception utterly unworthy of their character as sincere and honest men and patriots. It may, therefore, be fairly inferred that, retaining the same style, they intended to attach to the expression "the United States" the same meaning, substantially, which it previously had; and, of course, in calling the present government "the federal government of these States," they meant by "federal" that they stood in the same relation to each other—that their union rested, without material change, on the same basis—as under the Confederacy and the Revolutionary government, and that federal and confederated States meant substantially the same thing. It follows also that the changes made by the present Constitution were not in the foundation but in the superstructure of the system. We accordingly find, in confirmation of this conclusion, that the Convention, in their letter to Congress stating the reasons for the changes that had been made, refer only to the necessity which required a different *organization* of the government, without making any allusion whatever to any change in the relations of the States toward each other or the basis of the system. They state that—

the friends of our country have long seen and desired that the power of making war, peace, and treaties; that of levying money and regulating commerce, and the correspondent executive and judicial authorities, should be fully and effectually vested in the Government of the Union: but the impropriety of delegating such extensive trusts to one body of men is evident; hence results the necessity of a *different organization*.

Comment is unnecessary.

We thus have the authority of the Convention itself for asserting that the expression "United States" has essentially the same meaning, when applied to the present Constitution and government, as it had previously; and, of course, that the States have retained their separate existence as independent and sovereign communities in all the forms of political existence through which they have passed. Such, indeed, is the literal import of the expression "the United States," and the sense in which it is ever used when it is applied politically.

I say politically because it is often applied *geographically*
to designate the portion of this continent occupied by the
States composing the Union, including territories belonging
to them. This application arose from the fact that there was
no appropriate term for that portion of this continent; and
thus, not unnaturally, the name by which these States are
politically designated was employed to designate the region
they occupy and possess. The distinction is important and
cannot be overlooked in discussing questions involving the
character and nature of the government without causing great
confusion and dangerous misconceptions.

But as conclusive as these reasons are to prove that the
government of the United States is federal, in contradistinction to national, it would seem that they have not been sufficient to prevent the opposite opinion from being entertained.
Indeed, this last seems to have become the prevailing one, if
we may judge from the general use of the term "national"
and the almost entire disuse of that of "federal." "National"
is now commonly applied to "the general government of the
Union" and "the federal government of these States," and all
that appertains to them or to the Union. It seems to be for-
gotten that the term was repudiated by the Convention after
full consideration, and that it was carefully excluded from
the Constitution and the letter laying it before Congress.
Even those who know all this—and, of course, how falsely
the term is applied—have, for the most part, slided into its
use without reflection. But there are not a few who so apply
it because they believe it to be a national government in fact;
and among these are men of distinguished talents and standing, who have put forth all their powers of reason and elo-
quence in support of the theory. The question involved is
one of the first magnitude and deserves to be investigated
thoroughly in all its aspects. With this impression I deem it
proper—clear and conclusive as I regard the reasons already
assigned to prove its federal character—to confirm them by
historical references; and to repel the arguments adduced to
prove it to be a national government. I shall begin with the
formation and ratification of the Constitution.

That the States, when they formed and ratified the Constitution, were distinct, independent, and sovereign communities has already been established. That the people of the several States, acting in their separate, independent, and sovereign character, adopted their separate State constitutions is a fact uncontested and incontestable; but it is not more certain than that, acting in the same character, they ratified and adopted the Constitution of the United States; with this difference only, that in making and adopting the one, they acted without concert or agreement, but, in the other, with concert in making and mutual agreement in adopting it. That the delegates who constituted the Convention which framed the Constitution were appointed by the several States, each on its own authority; that they voted in the Convention by States; and that their votes were counted by States—are recorded and unquestionable facts. So, also, the facts that the Constitution, when framed, was submitted to the people of the several States for their respective ratification; that it was ratified by them, each for itself; and that it was binding on each, only in consequence of its being so ratified by it. Until then, it was but the plan of a constitution, without any binding force. It was the act of ratification which established it as a Constitution between the States ratifying it; and only between *them*, on the condition that not less than nine of the then thirteen States should concur in the ratification, as it expressly provided by its seventh and last Article. It is in the following words: "The ratification of the conventions of nine States shall be sufficient for the establishment of this Constitution between the States so ratifying the same." If additional proof be needed to show that it was only binding between the States that ratified it, it may be found in the fact that two States, North Carolina and Rhode Island, refused at first to ratify and were, in consequence, regarded in the interval as foreign States, without obligation on their parts to respect it, or, on the part of their citizens, to obey it. Thus far, there can be no difference of opinion. The facts are too recent and too well established, and the provision of the Constitution too explicit, to admit of doubt.

That the States, then, retained, after the ratification of the Constitution, the distinct, independent, and sovereign character in which they formed and ratified it is certain, unless they divested themselves of it by the act of ratification or by some provision of the Constitution. If they have not, the Constitution must be federal and not national; for it would have, in that case, every attribute necessary to constitute it federal, and not one to make it national. On the other hand, if they have divested themselves, then it would necessarily lose its federal character and become national. Whether, then, the government is federal or national is reduced to a single question: whether the act of ratification, of itself, or the Constitution, by some one or all of its provisions did, or did not, divest the several States of their character of separate, independent, and sovereign communities, and merge them all in one great community or nation, called the American people?

Before entering on the consideration of this important question, it is proper to remark that on its decision the character of the government, as well as the Constitution, depends. The former must, necessarily, partake of the character of the latter, as it is but its agent, created by it, to carry its powers into effect. Accordingly, then, as the Constitution is federal or national, so must the government be; and I shall, therefore, use them indiscriminately in discussing the subject.

Of all the questions which can arise under our system of government, this is by far the most important. It involves many others of great magnitude; and among them that of the allegiance of the citizen; or, in other words, the question to whom allegiance and obedience are ultimately due. What is the true relation between the two governments, that of the United States and those of the several States, and what is the relation between the individuals respectively composing them? For it is clear, if the States still retain their sovereignty as separate and independent communities, the allegiance and obedience of the citizens of each would be due to their respective States; and that the government of the United States and those of the several States would stand as equals and coordinates in their respective spheres; and, instead of being united socially, their citizens would be politically connected through their respective States. On the contrary, if they have, by ratifying the Constitution, divested themselves of their individuality and sovereignty, and merged themselves into one great community or nation, it is equally clear that the sovereignty would reside in the whole, or what is called the American people; and that allegiance and obedience would be due to them. Nor is it less so that the government of the several States would, in such case, stand to that of the United States in the relation of inferior and subordinate to superior and paramount; and that the individuals of the several States, thus fused, as it were, into one general mass would be united *socially* and not *politically*. So great a change of condition would have involved a thorough and radical revolution, both socially and politically —a revolution much more radical, indeed, than that which followed the Declaration of Independence.

They who maintain that the ratification of the Constitution effected so mighty a change are bound to establish it by the most demonstrative proof. The presumption is strongly opposed to it. It has already been shown that the authority of the Convention which formed the Constitution is clearly against it and that the history of its ratification, instead of supplying evidence in its favor, furnishes strong testimony in opposition to it. To these, others may be added, and among them the presumption drawn from the history of these States, in all the stages of their existence down to the time of the ratification of the constitution. In all, they formed separate and, as it respects each other, independent communities, and were ever remarkable for the tenacity with which they adhered to their rights as such. It constituted, during the whole period, one of the most striking traits in their character, as a very brief sketch will show.

During their colonial condition they formed distinct communities, each with its separate charter and government, and in no way connected with each other, except as dependent members of a common empire. Their first union among themselves was in resistance to the encroachments of the parent country on their chartered rights, when they adopted the title of "the United Colonies." Under that name they acted until they declared their independence—always, in their joint councils, voting and acting as separate and distinct communities, and not in the aggregate, as composing one community or nation. They acted in the same character in declaring independence, by which act they passed from their dependent, colonial condition into that of free and sovereign States. The Declaration was made by delegates appointed by the several colonies, each for itself and on its own authority. The vote making the Declaration was taken by delegations, each counting one. The Declaration was announced to be unanimous, not because every delegate voted for it, but because the majority of each delegation did; showing clearly that the body itself regarded it as the united act of the several colonies, and not the act of the whole as one community. To leave no doubt on a point so important and in reference to which the several colonies were so tenacious, the Declaration was made in the name and by the authority of the people of the colonies represented in Congress, and that was followed by declaring them to be "free and independent States." The act was, in fact, but a formal and solemn annunciation to the world that the colonies had ceased to be dependent communities and had become free and independent States, without involving any other change in their relations with each other than those necessarily incident to a separation from the parent country. So far were they from supposing or intending that it should have the effect of merging their existence as separate communities into one nation that they had appointed a committee, which was actually sitting while the declaration was under discussion, to prepare a plan of a confederacy of the States, preparatory to entering into their new condition. In fulfillment of their appointment, this committee prepared the draft of the Articles of Confederation and Perpetual Union, which afterward was adopted by the governments of the several States. That it instituted a mere confederacy and union of the States has already been shown. That, in forming and assenting to it, the States were exceedingly jealous and watchful in delegating power, even to a confederacy; that they granted the powers delegated most reluctantly and sparingly; that several of them long stood out, under all the pressure of the Revolutionary War, before they acceded to it; and that, during the interval which elapsed between its adoption and that of the present Constitution they evinced, under the most urgent necessity, the same reluctance and jealousy in delegating power—are facts which cannot be disputed.

To this may be added another circumstance of no little weight, drawn from the preliminary steps taken for the ratification of the constitution. The plan was laid, by the Convention, before the Congress of the Confederacy, for its consideration and action, as has been stated. It was the sole organ and representative of these States in their confederated character. By submitting it, the Convention recognized and acknowledged its authority over it as the organ of distinct, independent, and sovereign States. It had the right to dispose of it as it pleased; and, if it had thought proper, it might have defeated the plan by simply omitting to act on it. But it thought proper to act and to adopt the course recommended by the Convention, which was to submit it—"to a convention of delegates, chosen in each State, by the people thereof, for their assent and adoption." All this was in strict accord with the federal character of the Constitution, but wholly repugnant to the idea of its being national. It received the assent of the States in all the possible modes in which it could be obtained: first, in their confederated character, through its only appropriate organ, the Congress; next, in their individual character, as separate States, through their respective State governments to which the Congress referred it; and finally, in their high character of independent and sovereign communities, through a convention of the people called in each State, by the authority of its government. The States acting in these various capacities might, at every stage, have defeated it or not, at their option, by giving or withholding their consent.

With this weight of presumptive evidence, to use no stronger expression, in favor of its federal, in contradistinction to its national character, I shall next proceed to show that the ratification of the Constitution, instead of furnishing proof against, contains additional and conclusive evidence in its favor.

We are not left to conjecture as to what was meant by the ratification of the Constitution, or its effects. The expressions used by the conventions of the States in ratifying it and those used by the Constitution in connection with it afford ample means of ascertaining with accuracy both its meaning and effect. The usual form of expression used by the former is: "We, the delegates of the State (naming the State) do, in behalf of the people of the State, assent to and ratify the said Constitution." All use "ratify," and all except North Carolina use "assent to." The delegates of that State use "adopt" instead of "assent to"—a variance merely in the form of expression, without in any degree affecting the meaning. Ratification was, then, the act of the several States in their separate capacity. It was performed by delegates appointed expressly for the purpose. Each appointed its own delegates; and the delegates of each acted in the name of and for the State appointing them. Their act consisted in "assenting to" or, what is the same thing, "adopting and ratifying" the Constitution.

By turning to the Seventh Article of the Constitution and to the Preamble, it will be found what was the effect of ratifying. The Article expressly provides that, "the ratification of the conventions of nine States shall be sufficient for the establishment of this Constitution between the States so ratifying the same." The Preamble of the Constitution is in the following words:

We, the people of the United States, in order to form a more perfect union, establish justice, insure domestic tranquillity, provide for the common defence, promote the general welfare, and secure the blessings of liberty to ourselves and our posterity, do ordain and establish this Constitution for the United States of America.

The effect, then, of its ratification was, to ordain and establish the Constitution and thereby to make what was before but a plan—"The Constitution of the United States of America." All this is clear.

It remains now to show *by whom* it was ordained and established, *for whom* it was ordained and established, *for what* it was ordained and established, and *over whom* it was ordained and established. These will be considered in the order in which they stand.

Nothing more is necessary, in order to show by whom it was ordained and established, than to ascertain who are meant by "We, the people of the United States"; for, by their authority, it was done. To this there can be but one answer: it meant the people who ratified the instrument, for it was the act of ratification which ordained and established it. Who they were admits of no doubt. The process preparatory to ratification and the acts by which it was done prove, beyond the possibility of a doubt, that it was ratified by the several States, through conventions of delegates chosen in each State by the people thereof and acting, each in the name and by the authority of its State; and, as all the States ratified it, "We, the people of the United States," mean: We, the people of the several States of the Union. The inference is irresistible. And when it is considered that the States of the Union were then members of the Confederacy and that, by the express provision of one of its articles, "each State retains its sovereignty, freedom, and independence," the proof is demonstrative that "We, the people of the United States of America," mean the people of the several States of the Union, acting as free, independent, and sovereign States. This strikingly confirms what has been already stated, to wit, that the Convention which formed the Constitution meant the same thing by the terms "United States" and "federal," when applied to the Constitution or government; and that the former, when used politically, always mean these States united as independent and sovereign communities.

Having shown *by whom* it was ordained, there will be no difficulty in determining *for whom* it was ordained. The Preamble is explicit: it was ordained and established for "The United States of America," adding "America" in conformity to the style of the then Confederacy and the Declaration of Independence. Assuming, then, that the "United States" bears the same meaning in the conclusion of the Preamble as it does in its commencement (and no reason can be assigned why it should not), it follows necessarily that the Constitution was ordained and established *for* the people of the several States, *by* whom it was ordained and established.

Nor will there be any difficulty in showing *for what* it was ordained and established. The Preamble enumerates the objects. They are: "to form a more perfect union, to establish justice, insure domestic tranquillity, provide for the common defence, promote the general welfare, and secure the blessings of liberty to ourselves and our posterity." To effect these objects, they ordained and established, to use their own language, "the Constitution for the United States of America," clearly meaning by "for" that it was intended to be *their* Constitution; and that the objects of ordaining and establishing it were to perfect *their* union, to establish justice among *them*, to insure *their* domestic tranquillity, to provide for *their* common defence and general welfare, and to secure the blessings of liberty to *them* and *their* posterity. Taken all together, it follows from what has been stated that the Constitution was ordained and established *by* the several States as *distinct, sovereign communities*, and that it was ordained and established by them for *themselves*—for their common welfare and safety, as *distinct and sovereign communities*.

It remains to be shown *over whom* it was ordained and established. That it was not over *the several States* is settled by the Seventh Article beyond controversy. It declares that the ratification by nine States shall be sufficient to establish the Constitution between the States so ratifying. "Between" necessarily excludes "*over*," as that which is *between* States cannot be *over* them. Reason itself, if the Constitution had been silent, would have led with equal certainty to the same conclusion. For it was the several States, or, what is the same thing, their people, in their sovereign capacity, who ordained and established the Constitution. But the authority which ordains and establishes is higher than that which is ordained and established; and of course the latter must be subordinate to the former and cannot, therefore, be *over* it. "Between" always means more than "over" and implies in this case that the authority which ordained and established the Constitution was the joint and united authority of the States ratifying it; and that, among the effects of their ratification, it became a contract between them and, *as a compact,* binding on them—but only as such. In that sense the term "between" is appropriately applied. In no other can it be. It was doubtless used in that sense in this instance; but the question still remains *over whom* was it ordained and established? After what has been stated, the answer may be readily given. It was *over the government* which is created, and all its functionaries in their official character, and the individuals composing and inhabiting the several States, as far as they might come within the sphere of the powers delegated to the United States.

I have now shown conclusively, by arguments drawn from the act of ratification and the Constitution itself, that the several States of the Union, acting in their confederated character, ordained and established the Constitution; that they ordained and established it for themselves, in the same character; that they ordained and established it for their welfare and safety, in the like character; that they established it as a compact *between* them, and not as a constitution *over* them; and that, as a compact, they are parties to it, in the same character. I have thus established, conclusively, that these States, in ratifying the Constitution, did not lose the confederated character which they possessed when they ratified it, as well as in all the preceding stages of their existence; but, on the contrary, retained it to the full.

.   .   .   .

[A Plural Executive Proposed] [3]

In the meantime the spirit of fanaticism, which had been long lying dormant, was roused into action by the course of the government, as has been explained. It aims, openly and directly, at destroying the existing relations between the races in the southern section, on which depend its peace, prosperity, and safety. To effect this, exclusion from the territories is an important step; and hence the union between the abolitionists and the advocates of exclusion, to effect objects so intimately connected.

All this has brought about a state of things hostile to the continuance of the Union and the duration of the government. Alienation is succeeding to attachment, and hostile feelings to alienation; and these, in turn, will be followed by revolution or a disruption of the Union, unless timely prevented. But this cannot be done by restoring the government to its federal character, however necessary that may be as a first step. What has been done cannot be undone. The equilibrium between the two sections has been permanently destroyed by the measures above stated. The northern section, in consequence, will ever concentrate within itself the two majorities of which the government is composed; and should the southern be excluded from all territories now acquired, or to be hereafter acquired, it will soon have so decided a preponderance in the government and the Union as to be able to mold the Constitution to its pleasure. Against this, the restoration of the federal character of the government can furnish no remedy. So long as it continues, there can be no safety for the weaker section. It places in the hands of the stronger and hostile section the power to crush her and her institutions, and leaves her no alternative but to resist or sink down into a colonial condition. This must be the consequence, if some effectual and appropriate remedy be not applied.

[3] Crallé, *op. cit.*, Vol. I, pp. 390-395.

The nature of the disease is such that nothing can reach it, short of some organic change—a change which shall so modify the Constitution as to give to the weaker section, in some one form or another, a negative on the action of the government. Nothing short of this can protect the weaker, and restore harmony and tranquillity to the Union, by arresting effectually the tendency of the dominant and stronger section to oppress the weaker. When the Constitution was formed, the impression was strong that the tendency to conflict would be between the larger and smaller States, and effectual provisions were accordingly made to guard against it. But experience has proved this to have been a mistake; and that, instead of being as was then supposed, the conflict is between the two great sections, which are so strongly distinguished by their institutions, geographical character, productions and pursuits. Had this been then as clearly perceived as it now is, the same jealousy which so vigilantly watched and guarded against the danger of the larger States oppressing the smaller would have taken equal precaution to guard against the same danger between the two sections. It is for us who see and feel it to do what the framers of the Constitution would have done had they possessed the knowledge in this respect which experience has given to us, that is, provide against the dangers which the system has practically developed; and which, had they been foreseen at the time and left without guard, would undoubtedly have prevented the States, forming the southern section of the Confederacy, from ever agreeing to the Constitution; and which, under like circumstances, were they now out of, would prevent them from entering into the Union.

How the Constitution could best be modified, so as to effect the object, can only be authoritatively determined by the amending power. It may be done in various ways. Among others, it might be effected through a reorganization of the executive department; so that its powers, instead of being vested, as they now are, in a single officer, should be vested in two; to be so elected as that the two should be constituted the special organs and representatives of the respective sections in the executive department of the government, and requiring each to approve all the acts of Congress before they shall become laws. One might be charged with the administration of matters connected with the foreign relations of the country, and the other of such as were connected with its domestic institutions, the selection to be decided by lot. It would thus effect, more simply, what was intended by the original provisions of the Constitution, in giving to one of the majorities composing the government a decided preponderance in the Electoral College, and to the other majority a still more decided influence in the eventual choice in case the College failed to elect a President. It was intended to effect an equilibrium between the larger and smaller States in this department, but which, in practice, has entirely failed, and, by its failure, done much to disturb the whole system and to bring about the present dangerous state of things.

Indeed, it may be doubted whether the framers of the Constitution did not commit a great mistake in constituting a single instead of a plural executive. Nay, it may even be doubted whether a single chief magistrate—invested with all the power properly appertaining to the executive department of the government, as is the President—is compatible with the permanence of a popular government, especially in a wealthy and populous community, with a large revenue and a numerous body of officers and employees. Certain it is that there is no instance of a popular government so constituted which has long endured. Even ours, thus far, furnishes no evidence in its favor, and not a little against it; for to it the present disturbed and dangerous state of things, which threatens the country with monarchy or disunion, may be justly attributed. On the other hand, the two most distinguished constitutional governments of antiquity, both in respect to permanence and power, had a dual executive. I refer to those of Sparta and of Rome. The former had two hereditary, and the latter two elective chief magistrates. It is true that England, from which ours, in this respect, is copied, has a single hereditary head of the executive department of her government; but it is not less true that she has had many and arduous struggles to prevent her chief magistrate from becoming absolute, and that, to guard against it effectually, she was finally compelled to divest him substantially of the power of administering the government by transferring it, practically, to a cabinet of responsible ministers, who, by established custom, cannot hold office unless supported by a majority of the two houses of Parliament. She has thus avoided the danger of the chief magistrate becoming absolute and contrived to unite, substantially, a single with a plural executive, in constituting that department of her government. We have no such guard, and can have none such without an entire change in the character of our government; and her example, of course, furnishes no evidence in favor of a single chief magistrate in a popular form of government like ours —while the example of former times, and our own thus far, furnish strong evidence against it.

But it is objected that a plural executive necessarily leads to intrigue and discord among its members, and that it is inconsistent with prompt and efficient action. This may be true when they are all elected by the same constituency and may be a good reason, where this is the case, for preferring a single executive, with all its objections, to a plural executive. But the case is very different where they are elected by different constituencies having conflicting and hostile interests, as would be the fact in the case under consideration. Here the two would have to act concurringly in approving the acts of Congress and separately in the sphere of their respective departments. The effect, in the latter case, would be to retain all the advantages of a single executive, as far as the administration of the laws were concerned; and, in the former, to insure harmony and concord between the two sections and, through them, in the government. For as no act of Congress could become a law without the assent of the chief magistrates representing both sections, each, in the elections, would choose the candidate who, in addition to being faithful to its interests, would best command the esteem and confidence of the other section. And thus the Presidential election, instead of dividing the Union into hostile geographical parties—the stronger struggling to enlarge its powers, and the weaker to defend its rights, as is now the case—would become the means of restoring harmony and concord to the country and the government. It would make the Union a union in truth— a bond of mutual affection and brotherhood—and not a mere connection used by the stronger as the instrument of dominion and aggrandizement, and submitted to by the weaker only from the lingering remains of former attachment and the fading hope of being able to restore the government to what it was originally intended to be, a blessing to all.

.   .   .   .